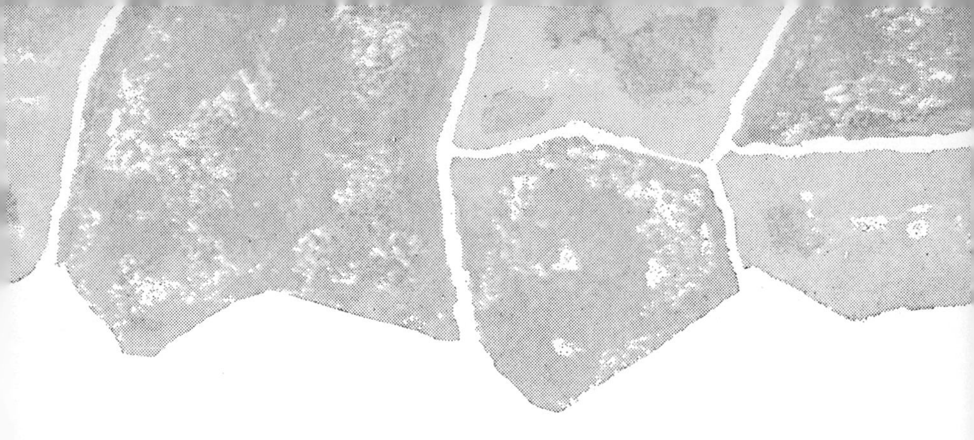

ART BY SUBTRACTION

A Dissenting Opinion of Gertrude Stein

ART BY

SUBTRACTION

A Dissenting Opinion of Gertrude Stein

BY B. L. REID

University of Oklahoma Press: Norman

The publication of this work
has been aided by a grant from
THE FORD FOUNDATION

Library of Congress Catalog Card Number: 58–6852

Composed and printed at Norman, Oklahoma, U.S.A.,
by the University of Oklahoma Press.
First edition.

TO ETHEL

AND SARAH T. RAMAGE

PREFACE

This book is born of a gradual disenchantment, and I suppose it finally amounts to an essay in decapitation—without acrimony, but with conviction. I was moved and instructed by Gertrude Stein's *Three Lives* and amused and excited by her *Autobiography of Alice B. Toklas,* the two most commonly available of her books. The experience was sharp enough to make me want to read deeper in her work and, eventually, in what the critics had to say about her. Deeper reading convinced me of several facts I had not expected, which, in combination, seemed themselves worth writing about: *Three Lives* and *The Autobiography of Alice B. Toklas* give one a very deceptive sample of Gertrude Stein's actual character as a writer; Miss Stein has been given remarkably little perceptive criticism, and she occupies her literary position partly because of this default of criticism; the aesthetic problems raised by her writing are difficult and important enough and little enough understood to deserve a thoughtful examination at some length.

In this study I have tried to shed some light on these matters and to arrive at a personal critical stand on the issues raised by Gertrude Stein's writing. I begin with a chapter surveying her critics and close with a long chapter of evaluation; the chapters in between, the bulk of the book, are analytical and expository. I have placed most of my value judgments in the long last chapter, building and supporting them slowly in the analytical chapters that precede. I am sure, as I have intimated, that Gertrude Stein has been overvalued as a writer, but only great care entitles us to be careless at last.

Now, a dozen years after Gertrude Stein's death and more than half a century after she began writing, a number of recent publishing events advertise us that she is not to be allowed to disappear quickly. In 1950 the Banyan Press brought out in a luxury edition Miss Stein's "forgotten" first novel under the title *Things as They Are*. Beginning in 1951, the Yale University Press has issued annually a new volume mined from Miss Stein's unpublished writings; the eighth and final volume in the series will appear in 1958. In 1951, Yale issued Donald Sutherland's excellent study, *Gertrude Stein: A Biography of Her Work,* which remains the only roundly satisfying work of criticism addressed to Miss Stein. In 1957 appeared Elizabeth Sprigge's *Gertrude Stein: Her Life and Work,* the first moderately full-dress treatment of the life from the outside. This sizable flurry surely indicates confidence in respected quarters that Miss Stein's work is still worth quantities of paper, ink, and time. I spend the same ingredients here because it seems worth while to doubt that judgment publicly and to suggest that serious acceptance of writing which seems to me ultimately unserious is wasteful of time we need for reading toward richer increment.

It appears that Mr. Sutherland's book is to stand in the Yale Stein series as the official "biography of her work." For the sake of Miss Stein's reputation it is a fortunate choice, and readers who want to see the assenting opinion in a superbly just and literate form should turn to this volume and to Mr. Sutherland's preface to the sixth of the posthumous volumes from Yale, *Stanzas in Meditation*. Mr. Sutherland's defense is meaty, eloquent, perspicuous, and wide in range, fully learned in Miss Stein's writing and in literature generally. My own particular bias leads me to think that his major conclusions are in error and that details of his argument are specious and deceptive. The basic disagreement is just that—a disagreement concerning the real status of writing in our time and the real value of Gertrude Stein's peculiarities of composition. Certain it is, at any rate, that the true critical issue raised by her work is fully and intelligently joined for the first time in his book.

Had I known Gertrude Stein, as did most of those who have written well about her—Thornton Wilder and Carl Van Vechten and Donald Sutherland, for example—

my final critical judgments might well have been less positive and less heavy footed than they now are. Not to have known her is indeed in one sense a disqualification, since so much of her contemporary force has been that of her powerful presence. In another sense, not to have known her personally may be a positive qualification of some value; it was as a writer that she wanted to live, and doubtless it is easier, if duller, to focus on her printed page when one is not distracted by her ingratiating and forceful image.

B. L. REID

South Hadley, Massachusetts
February 18, 1958

CONTENTS

ILLUSTRATIONS

ART BY SUBTRACTION

A Dissenting Opinion of Gertrude Stein

. . . you never want to use anything but white keys black keys are too harmonious and you never want to do a chord chords are too emotional, you want to use white keys and play two hands together but not bother which direction either hand takes not at all you want to make it like a design and always looking and you will have a good time.

—*Everybody's Autobiography*

Bear it in your mind my reader, but truly I never feel it that there ever can be for me any such a creature, no it is this scribbled and dirty and lined paper that is to be to me always my receiver.

—*The Making of Americans*

1

GERTRUDE STEIN'S CRITICS

The critics, by and large, have fled from Gertrude Stein. I doubt that any other modern writer so widely considered important has received so little competent criticism, whether it is measured qualitatively or quantitatively. For example, she has not had one-tenth the volume of commentary that has been allotted to James Joyce, with whom she is often vaguely—and wrongly—coupled. This seems to me perfectly just: Joyce is ten times the greater artist. What I am anxious to note here is the startling disparity between Gertrude Stein's commentary and her popular reputation. One can still name on the fingers of one hand the thoughtful, extended treatments of her work: Donald Sutherland's *Gertrude Stein: A Biography of Her Work*, Edmund Wilson's essay in *Axel's Castle*, Robert Haas's introduction to *What Are Masterpieces*, and Thornton Wilder's fine introduction to *Four in America*. One might also include W. G. Rogers' *When This You See Remember Me*, Julian Sawyer's preface to his excellent *Bibliography*, and Elizabeth Sprigge's *Gertrude Stein: Her Life and Her Work*. But Rogers' work is really a book-length memoir published soon after Miss Stein's death and seems to me largely "occasional" and only incidentally and unprofoundly critical. Sawyer's preface is intermittently enligthening, but generally it has interest only as a case history of the kind of imbalance Gertrude Stein induced in her more perfervid votaries. Miss Sprigge's new biography is a clear and orderly collection of largely familiar data, but it is of no help as criticism.

Although this general critical picture is at first surprising, it is nonetheless easy to understand. Very few writers—perhaps none—have presented the critics with so many difficult problems in evaluation. The first printed criticism of Miss Stein's work I have been able to find makes this cautious judgment:

> *. . . readers who are willing to pay a stiff entrance fee in patient attention may learn for themselves. From Miss Stein, if she can consent to clarify her method, much may be expected.*[1]

This critic was balking thus mildly at *Three Lives*; the reader who believes that book exacts a "stiff entrance fee" should try *Geography and Plays*, or, better yet, *The Making of Americans*. For, of course, Gertrude Stein did not

[1] "Three Lives," *Nation*, Vol. XC (January 20, 1910), 65.

"consent to clarify her method"; she became steadily more difficult, and *Three Lives* eventually comes to seem classically simple.

5 Even the critic who balks more boldly at Miss Stein, daring to brave the charges of arrant Philistinism that are sure to be leveled by her admirers, must puzzle his way through many textual difficulties and problems of personality. To put the case bluntly, how, in the first place, to understand what she is talking about in a great portion of her work? How to reconcile the coexistence in most of her books of the deeply perceptive, the incomprehensible, the comprehensible but worthless? How to reconcile a fine book such as *Three Lives* with a trivial one such as *The Geographical History of America?* How to mediate between one's own impression of the shallowness of much of her writing and the testimony of many intelligent persons to her "genius"? How to separate the personality from the art? How, particularly, to keep the image of that magnificent head (the head like Caesar's, somebody called it) from intruding upon one's judgments? Such questions continually plague the critic; the difficulties are real enough. Whatever the reason, the point is that she holds her place largely unread and uncriticized.

Nor is it hard to understand why criticism of Gertrude Stein has tended, in one direction or another, to hyperbole. Moderation is scarcely to be expected in readers of a lifework so huge, so strange, so remorselessly difficult. One does not temporize with a writer like Miss Stein, and many critics have treated her not unjustifiably in an all-

or-nothing manner. In one sense the critic has to accept Gertrude Stein as a genius or refuse her as a fool: she cannot be both pigmy and giant. But it is surely regrettable that so many of her critics have assumed such positions without sufficient buttressing in textual evidence. Again and again one has the feeling that a given judgment of Miss Stein has not grown out of an intimate knowledge of the work at hand, but out of mere sympathy with an attitude dimly felt in her work or out of ignorance or bewilderment. Too often we find no truly critical weighing and measuring, but the "flattery or intimidation" that Desmond MacCarthy calls "the method of imperfectly convinced critics."[2] Far too much of the judgment of Gertrude Stein falls into these two schools of imperfect conviction; the critic may adore or vilify her, but he usually does so in a manner that begs the question; he makes his points by shouting. The disinterested judge can ask in all fairness whether or not Miss Stein has really been read.

Perhaps the best way to survey Gertrude Stein's critics is to look briefly at the two extremes, the hyperbolic schools of adoration and vilification, trying only to have a good time, then take a longer look at the soberer judgments, concentrating on the best of them, the essays by Edmund Wilson and Thornton Wilder and the book by Donald Sutherland.

Because Miss Stein's imperfectly convinced critics have had to resort to various stratagems to cover the poverty of their critical evidence, some rather amusing pat-

[2] Desmond MacCarthy, "Gertrude Stein," in *Criticism,* 271.

terns begin to appear. Most reviews rely heavily on quotation; many fall back, sometimes consciously and sometimes not, on imitation that occasionally amounts to downright parody of Miss Stein's style of the moment; many make ingenious comparisons with the work of other writers or with nonsense material; metaphor is likely to be superabundant. As many as possible manage to include a photograph of her clear-eyed, good-humored, obviously intelligent face—which always makes its own forceful argument, regardless of the opinion of the critic. One very significant fact emerges: Gertrude Stein's most ardent champions are those who have come, in some degree, under the sway of her personality.

Let us begin with something like the ultimate. Julian Sawyer stated in 1940 that Gertrude Stein was "the most important writer writing today";[3] in 1933, Bernard Fay, Miss Stein's French translator, believed her to be "the most intelligent American woman alive at present"[4] (but some of the force of this remark evaporates when we encounter Perry Miller's opinion that Fay himself is "one of Europe's leading charlatans"[5]). Louis Bromfield tempers the general extravagance in calling Miss Stein "the clearest intelligence I have ever encountered."[6] Bromfield

[3] Julian Sawyer, *Gertrude Stein: A Bibliography*, 30.

[4] Bernard Fay, "A Rose Is a Rose," *Saturday Review of Literature*, Vol. X (September 2, 1933), 79.

[5] Perry Miller, "Steinese," *New York Times Book Review*, November 3, 1946, p. 30.

[6] Louis Bromfield, "Gertrude Stein, Experimenter With Words," *New York Herald Tribune Books*, September 3, 1933, p. 1.

also joins in a fairly widespread judgment of her influence on American writing:

. . . it has set aside American writing . . . from all others in this century. Today one can pick up a book and by the writing *of the page tell whether it is written by an American or an Englishman. It seems to me that one powerful influence, emanating from 27 rue de Fleurus, is largely responsible.*[7]

Dudley Fitts found her a "consummate artist and profound intelligence."[8] Leo Lerman believed that Gertrude Stein "practically invented today in literature."[9] And this passage from the same essay can stand as a good example of the style derived from her and of the double talk and evasion of a critic's job of work which so often followed Miss Stein:

But some could see with their ears and smell with their eyes and taste with their whole selves. And they knew what she was saying and that it was important.

So now she has departed but she is here and everyone who writes must be more explicit because of her writing both intelligibly and unintelligibly.[10]

Joseph Alsop was one of the few who knew Ger-

7 *Ibid.*
8 Dudley Fitts, "Toasted Susie Is My Ice-Cream," *New York Times Book Review,* November 30, 1947, p. 5.
9 Leo Lerman, "A Wonderchild for 72 Years," *Saturday Review of Literature,* Vol. XXIX (November 2, 1946), 18.
10 *Ibid.*

trude Stein well yet retained the capacity to evaluate her objectively. To him she seemed "no out-pensioner upon Parnassus; no crank; no seeker after personal publicity; no fool . . . a remarkably shrewd woman, with an intelligence both sensitive and tough."[11] He then proceeded to the conclusion that her only really important work was *Three Lives* and that her other works were marred by her denial of the need to communicate. This view strikes me as absolutely tenable, for reasons which I hope to make slowly clear in later chapters.

Gertrude Stein's detractors are, by and large, more amusing than her admirers, either for the heat generated in diatribe or for the wit and the flights of rhetoric and metaphor to which she inspired them. To begin again with something close to the ultimate, this time an assassination, we have Oscar Cargill's opinion that she was "the supreme egocentric of the most perfect clique of egocentrics."[12] Cargill, however, reserved a tremendous respect for "Melanctha," the most striking of the *Three Lives*. Ben Ray Redman ventured that "it is probable that no one else has ever written so much while saying so little."[13] For metaphor we may cite the *New Statesman's* comparison of Gertrude Stein to "an indefatigable little paddle-steamer caught in an ocean of molasses."[14] For rhetorical heat

[11] Joseph Alsop, "Gertrude Stein on Writing," *New York Herald Tribune Books*, January 10, 1937, p. 2.
[12] Oscar Cargill, "The Decadents," in *Intellectual America*, 283.
[13] Ben Ray Redman, "Word-Intoxicated Woman," *Saturday Review of Literature*, Vol. XXXII (April 2, 1949), 18.
[14] "Useful Knowledge," *New Statesman*, Vol. XXXIII (April 13, 1929), 22.

we have Myra Marini's review of *The Geographical History of America:*

Are there still people so impressed by the oracular—who really are so simpleminded that they dare not challenge the unintelligible? Are there still any to do honor to the gibbering ghosts of a dead era?[15]

Sylva Norman, reviewing Miss Stein's *Useful Knowledge,* was moved to a colder rage:

If Miss Stein's useful knowledge points out anything, it is that the loafing mind, equipped with language, can reach a triumph of chaotic imbecility.[16]

There is something of the true hyperbole, the authentic folk note, in random opinions like this:

After a hundred lines of this [Portrait of Mabel Dodge] *I wish to scream, I wish to burn the book, I am in agony. . . . Someone has applied an egg-beater to my brain.*[17]

Clifton Fadiman also aligned himself with the folk tradition; his opinion is perhaps characteristic enough of the labored witticism, with a nub of truth, that Miss Stein sometimes elicited to be worth quoting at some length:

[15] Myra Marini, "Being Dead Is Something," *New Republic,* Vol. LXXXIX (January 20, 1939), 365.
[16] Sylva Norman, "Words and Waste," *Nation and Athenaeum,* Vol. XLV (April 13, 1929), 52.
[17] "Flat Prose," *Atlantic Monthly,* Vol. CXIV (September, 1914), 432.

Portrait of Gertrude Stein 1907. From a painting by Felix Vallotton in the Cone Collection, Baltimore Museum of Art.

Gertrude Stein's Studio, 27 rue de Fleurus, Paris, about 1907. Courtesy Yale University Library

Gertrude Stein in 1937.

Courtesy Imogen Cunningham

Courtesy Yale University Library

Gertrude Stein in 1945.

> *My notion is that Miss Stein has set herself to solve, and has succeeded in solving, the most difficult problem in prose composition—to write something that will not arrest the attention in any way, manner, shape, or form. If you think this easy, try it. I know of no one except Miss Stein who can roll out this completely non-resistant prose, prose that puts you at once in a condition resembling the early stages of grippe—the eyes and legs heavy, the top of the skull wandering around in an uncertain and independent manner, the heart ponderously, tiredly beating. Take a sentence at random. . . . See what I mean? Sleep tight.*[18]

A number of nonsensical comparisons, funny and unfunny in varying proportions, have been inspired by Gertrude Stein's writing. A writer in the *Atlantic* compared her work to the song of a robin, with its "nuances of unintelligibility, symphonies of monotonous notes, *bravuras* of aimless repetition."[19] Desmond MacCarthy collated a Stein passage and one from a practice manual for typists and concluded that the two were equally worthless as art.[20] Max Eastman introduced excerpts from the writing of an insane person (taken from Kraepelin's *Clinical Psychology*).[21] Burton Rascoe devoted most of a "re-

[18] Clifton Fadiman, "Getting Gertie's Ida," *New Yorker*, Vol. XVII (February 15, 1941), 66.

[19] "Gertrude Stein and a Robin," *Atlantic Monthly*, Vol. CXXXIII (March, 1924), 427.

[20] MacCarthy, *op. cit.*, 261.

[21] Max Eastman, "The Cult of Unintelligibility," in *The Literary Mind*, 63.

view" of *Everybody's Autobiography* to the pidgin nonsense of a Japanese houseboy, one Hashimura Togo.[22]

Stuart Pratt Sherman engineered an experiment athletic and ingenious enough to deserve a separate paragraph here. He wrote down, he says, some one hundred words on a sheet of paper, cut them apart, separated them into piles according to parts of speech, shuffled them, and then aligned them and inserted punctuation—coming up, he says, with the following:

Red stupidity; but go slowly. The hope slim. Drink gloriously! Dream! Swiftly pretty people through daffodils slip in green doubt. Grandly fly bitter fish; for hard sunlight lazily consumes old books. Up by a sedate sweet heart roar darkly loud orchards. Life, the purple flame, simply proclaims a poem.[23]

Sherman concluded:

. . . my "work" made hers seem gray and protoplasmic.

It is necessary, therefore, to discard the theory that her book (Geography and Plays) *was written by any kind of mechanical device. It seems almost impossible by any unimpeded mechanical process to assort words in such a fashion that no glimmer of mind will flash out from their*

[22] Burton Rascoe, "Self-Confidential," *Saturday Review of Literature*, Vol. XVII (December 4, 1937), 11.

[23] Stuart Pratt Sherman, "A Note on Gertrude Stein," in *Points of View*, 267.

casual juxtapositions. The thing can be done only by unremitting intelligence of the first order.[24]

13 Two statements from Henry Seidel Canby can serve as examples of Gertrude Stein's effect on the conservative academic critic, thin but trying hard to be fair minded. His first dismissal of her in his *American Estimates* is complete but good humored:

> *The giants are often like that, especially in a period of decadence and affectation. Their obfuscations and great motions never carried through touch the imaginations of men wearied by the shining lucidities of the gods. They have attempted new things and the wise may learn of them, but for the foolish they are illusion, delusion, and confusion. When, blundering up the slopes of Olympus, they murmur with Miss Stein . . . may Lewis Carroll be there on the ramparts, to take his vorpal sword in hand and smite the frumious Bandersnatches!*[25]

Five years later, however, Mr. Canby had lost all patience: "This is an insult to the civilizations that with incredible labor united . . . sound and sense."[26]

Conrad Aiken, a better critic and himself one of the early scouts for modernism, proved the range of his toler-

[24] *Ibid.*, 268.
[25] Henry Seidel Canby, "Style in English," in *American Estimates*, 176–77.
[26] Henry Seidel Canby, "Cheating at Solitaire," *Saturday Review of Literature*, Vol. XI (November 17, 1934), 290.

ance when he described "Melanctha" and *The Autobiography of Alice B. Toklas* as "perfectly orthodox," but he could not stomach *The Making of Americans.* He found it

> . . . *a fantastic kind of disaster. . . . Miss Stein falls into a tireless and inert repetitiveness which becomes as stupefying as it is unintelligible. The famous "subtlety of rhythm" simply is not there: one could better find it in a tom-tom. The phrasing is almost completely unsensory, flat and colorless.*[27]

Now I should move upward a degree from this comparatively superficial "review" level of criticism—about which one can only say at last that it is sparse, extremist, and, for the most part, tedious and ill informed—in order to point to a number of critics who have written brief but perceptive essays on Gertrude Stein. In this connection I would mention particularly Kenneth Burke, William Troy, Harvey Eagleson, Max Eastman, and F. Cudworth Flint. None of these men makes the attempt to subsume any large portion of Miss Stein's aesthetics or her writings, but all of them have intelligent things to say. Eastman[28] and Eagleson[29] have both called attention sharply to her failure to communicate—which is indeed

[27] Conrad Aiken, "We Ask for Bread," *New Republic,* Vol. XXVIII (April 4, 1934), 219.
[28] Eastman, *op. cit.,* 57–66.
[29] Harvey Eagleson, "Gertrude Stein: Method in Madness," *Sewanee Review,* Vol. XLIV (April, 1936), 164–77.

the crime for which we shall finally have to hang her. Mr. Flint arrives at one of the more profound truths about Gertrude Stein when he discusses her "attempt to force a temporal art to produce effects proper to a spatial art."[30] It is only in such conceptual and comparative terms, it seems to me, that she can be rightly understood and justly valued. I find Mr. Flint's summary estimate of Gertrude Stein critically sound. He treats her as fundamentally a phenomenon, curious and of passing importance, one to be noticed with interest and rejected regretfully because she has the wrong answer to the right problem:

> *One must regard Miss Stein as something of a sorceress—a frank sorceress, eminently agreeable to expounding, to the profit of her audience, the secrets of her sorcery; but in the long run a person from whom one must escape.*[31]

Kenneth Burke has grappled with Gertrude Stein on at least four occasions, and each time he has put his mind to work on the problem to a degree comparatively rare in Stein criticism. Mr. Burke applies himself to the text of Miss Stein's books, resisting the influence of the sensationalism and personality seduction that have grown up around her name, and emerges with hard-headed and genuinely critical dicta. Like Mr. Flint, Burke notes the vital fact that Gertrude Stein makes radical departures

[30] F. Cudworth Flint, "Contemporary Criticism," *Southern Review*, Vol. II (1936–1937), 208–13.
[31] *Ibid.*, 212.

from her basic medium; as he puts it, she is "violating her genre" by ignoring "the inherent property of words: that quality in the literary man's medium which makes him start out with a definiteness that the other arts do not possess."[32] I should say that Kenneth Burke is very close in this statement to the precise center of Miss Stein's heresy, and I will go into this matter at length later. It is also Kenneth Burke who supplies me with the broadly useful phrase, "art by subtraction"; he applies it in comparing lines of Miss Stein's and Milton's in order to dramatize the poverty that follows from her habit of minimizing visible subject matter. Burke, by the way, falls into the almost universal error of overestimating her orientation to music.

There are a number of reasons why Edmund Wilson's essay in *Axel's Castle* is among the most interesting treatments of Gertrude Stein. In the first place, it is singular that he found her respectable company for Yeats, Joyce, Eliot, Proust, and Paul Valéry—although in so doing he was subscribing to a rating of Miss Stein that is fairly common. This was probably the first time she had been given so high a position by a first-rate critic. In all fairness, however, it should be remembered that in the end Wilson believed her to be distinctly inferior to his other personages as an artist—more like them in kind than in quality. But I am sure that he erred in finding even this limited likeness. Wilson includes Gertrude Stein as being, like the

[32] Kenneth Burke, "Engineering With Words," *Dial*, Vol. LXXIV (April, 1923), 410.

others, one whose work had been "largely a continuance or extension of Symbolism."[33] But Gertrude Stein was like these writers neither in kind nor in quality, and to see her as one who practiced an art that aimed in any way "to approximate the indefiniteness of music,"[34] to evoke by suggestion, is to make a serious mistake. Thus I should say that Wilson's essay is interesting, in the second place, as a case history of charitable error, of the ease with which Miss Stein's literary intentions can be misunderstood, even by a good critic. Finally, the essay reproduces a typical pattern-reaction to Gertrude Stein, the one that begins in enchantment and ends in complete disenchantment, doubling back then to the consolation of the quality of her mind and her personality, if not of her art.

In point of fact, Wilson's admiration is confined to *Three Lives*. He grows progressively more uncomfortable with her later works, so very uncomfortable that he seems almost to repent the whole project; more than half the essay relates only tangentially to Gertrude Stein. Specific treatment of her merges into an examination of the general theory of nonsense language and finally into a note on Dadaism.

But of *Three Lives* Edmund Wilson is enormously appreciative. He feels that there Gertrude Stein has "caught the very rhythms and accents of the minds of her heroines," and that "Melanctha" is "one of the best attempts of a white American novelist to understand the

[33] Edmund Wilson, "Gertrude Stein," in *Axel's Castle*, 24.
[34] *Ibid.*, 13.

mind of the modern Americanized negro."[35] He feels in Miss Stein a "masterly grasp of the organisms, contradictory and indissoluble, which human personalities are."[36] Wilson saw, as no one else had seen, that the controlling discipline of *Three Lives* was the conception of character on the basis of its division into fundamental personality types. Thereby he cleared the way for us to see that the central intention of that book was actually the same as that of *The Making of Americans*—that the second book was merely the first, writ enormously large and abstract.

When he comes to *The Making of Americans* Mr. Wilson makes the extraordinary confession—probably not as usual among critics as it ought to be—that he has not read all the book. Indeed he wonders whether it is possible to read it all. We should forgive him. The complete *Making of Americans* is, I am convinced, unreadable for a normal mind. I have read every word of the shortened version (I think I have—it's hard to be sure), but I am not proud of the accomplishment, and I doubt that a score of people could be found who have done even that. Wilson's final disillusionment is well begun here:

> *. . . already some ruminative self-hypnosis, some progressive slowing up of the mind, has begun to show itself in Miss Stein's work as a fatty degeneration of her imagination and style.*[37]

[35] *Ibid.*, 237–38.
[36] *Ibid.*, 238.
[37] *Ibid.*, 239.

But Gertrude Stein's mind was not, in fact, slowing up; it was merely finding its true bent. Her mind never really slowed up; it merely became progressively more complex and idiosyncratic until at last there was no single mind, let alone group of minds, to which it could communicate effectively. She had begun her great withdrawal into the closet of private art, the isolation that she herself could never understand.

Mr. Wilson's prime misreading of Gertrude Stein's literary aim, at any rate, is contained in his judgment of the language of her later work:

> *She has outdistanced any of the Symbolists in using words for pure purposes of suggestion—she has gone so far that she no longer even suggests.*[38]

Miss Stein, however, was never concerned with infusing her words with suggestion. She was "possessed with the intellectual passion for exactitude in description."[39] She considered her language rigidly denotative. She worked not for the proliferation of association of the Symbolists, but for "the destruction of associational emotion in poetry and prose."[40] By her own private definition, she was far closer in aim to the Naturalists, against whom the Symbolists revolted, than to the Symbolists themselves. So Edmund Wilson, though perfectly sound in his judgment

[38] *Ibid.*, 243.
[39] Gertrude Stein, *The Autobiography of Alice B. Toklas*, 174.
[40] *Ibid.*

of the value of her works as art, yet seems to have been almost completely mistaken in his reading of their aesthetic direction. I go into the matter at this length only because we may learn by his error.

Mr. Wilson's concluding estimate of Gertrude Stein's role in twentieth-century writing should be quoted in full, I think, because of its indication of his own final position, because of its clarity, and because of the fact that it reproduces so exactly the characteristic summary opinion of the balanced critics of her work:

> *Most of us balk at her soporific rigmaroles, her echolaliac incantations, her half-witted-sounding catalogues of numbers; most of us read her less and less. Yet, remembering especially her early work, we are still aware of her presence in the background of contemporary literature—and we picture her as the great pyramidal Buddha of Jo Davidson's statue of her, eternally and placidly ruminating the gradual developments of the processes of being, registering the vibrations of a psychological country like some august human seismograph whose charts we haven't the training to read. And whenever we pick up her writings, however unintelligible we may find them, we are aware of a literary personality of unmistakable originality and distinction.*[41]

Until the appearance of Donald Sutherland's book, Thornton Wilder's introduction to *Four in America* was by all odds the most illuminating approach to Gertrude

[41] Wilson, *op. cit.*, 252–53.

Stein that had yet been written, and it is still much the best short treatment. It is to be recommended to anyone seriously interested in this difficult woman. Mr. Wilder,
21 like Edmund Wilson, is a highly civilized man, and he writes with the added advantage of a long and intimate friendship with Miss Stein. As exegesis, it is hard to see how Mr. Wilder's twenty-two-page essay could be improved. As rounded criticism, on the other hand, the essay has, I feel, a fairly serious limitation: it is fundamentally apologia and appreciation. Mr. Wilder sees the whole truth about Gertrude Stein, or as much of it as anybody will ever see, but I think that his deep feeling for her as a person leads him to underestimate the limitations of her art, and in his admiration he occasionally mistakes the intention for the achievement.

Wilder's essay not only helps greatly to clarify Gertrude Stein's aims and practices, but also provides an invaluable record of the reaction of a sensitive and sympathetic mind to Miss Stein the person. Wilder's pages are filled with wonderful pictures of her gestures, her voice, her laughter, her humor, tolerance, force, and insight. No matter what one's prejudices, one can hardly leave the essay without feeling that Gertrude Stein was in many ways a very great lady and that she was engaged, with enormous intelligence and some humility, in a lifework of originality and human importance.

I have said that Thornton Wilder sees the truth about Gertrude Stein; he sees, in fact, what seem to me the two basic truths: that she is first of all a philosopher and aesthetician; that as an artist she has extreme limitations. He gives us this opinion:

I think it can be said that the fundamental occupation of Miss Stein's life was not the work of art but the shaping of a theory of knowledge, a theory of time, and a theory of the passions.[42]

At another point he sees in her "a passion to reduce the multitudinous occasions of the daily life to psychological and philosophical laws."[43] On the score of her limitations as an artist, Wilder deals only with the communication problem—central though it is:

She pursued her aims . . . with such conviction and intensity that occasionally she forgot that the results could be difficult to others.[44]
To her their meaning [*of her private locutions*] *is "self-evident"; she forgets that we have not participated in the systematic meditation that was her life.*[45]

Mr. Wilder is surely too mild here. The thing he is willing to minimize as "forgetting" is not really a forgivable trait in an artist. A good writer has the right to be occasionally or even frequently unintelligible and to de-

[42] Thornton Wilder, Introduction to *Four in America,* by Gertrude Stein, x.
[43] *Ibid.,* xv.
[44] *Ibid.,* v.
[45] *Ibid.,* xxii.

mand that we grow to apprehend him. Who has not been
often bewildered by Shakespeare, Donne, Blake, Yeats,
Joyce, Eliot? But Gertrude Stein's case is not theirs. There
23 is a difference between being difficult and being incom-
prehensible, just as, as Gertrude Stein was fond of insisting, there is a difference between a hysteric and a saint. The question is one of both degree and necessity. Miss Stein bewilders us in most of her serious writing—and that after hard and sympathetic reading. The productive idiosyncrasy of great minds is a marvelous fact; it forces us to gain stature in order to close the gap between them and us; it is illumination, the more powerful for being delayed. With Miss Stein too often the illumination never comes, or if we do finally labor into the light, we find it feeble; we find the obscurity to have been merely perverse, a trick of technique not inherent in the real stubbornness of the content, a trick practiced for her benefit—not ours.

The general excellence of Mr. Wilder's essay forms, in fact, a painful and instructive contrast to the text of the book it prefaces. It is sad that Gertrude Stein could not have reconciled herself to the only language in which she could have spoken to us; sad indeed that a long lifetime devoted to "knowledge, time and the passions" should be so largely wasted. It seems to me ironically true that the writing in this life devoted to writing has little value. The only people to whom Miss Stein left a real legacy were those lucky ones who knew her in person, those who

. . . came up to Paris "to see the Eiffel Tower and Gertrude Stein." They called and found bent upon them those gay and challenging eyes and that attention that asked nothing less of them than their genius.[46]

Since I shall make frequent reference to Donald Sutherland's views on Gertrude Stein as I develop my own argument, I shall give them less space here than they would otherwise deserve. His volume is the first, I think, in which Gertrude Stein has been offered the courtesy of full and informed attention. Let me establish my two main feelings about the book before going any further. I found it an extremely impressive piece of writing and thinking, perhaps the best existing defense of extreme abstractionism in literature, and a work which could easily find a permanent place in twentieth-century aesthetics. However, I believe that Mr. Sutherland's value judgments are in error and that in spite of much loving care he still fails, through faults of emphasis or proportion and the use of the often obscurative chronological attack, to make Gertrude Stein's aims genuinely clear, although he certainly leaves them clearer than they have ever been before. The volume is finely urbane, composed with care and balance, and written in prose of much grace and ease. It is complicated, in the best sense, functionally—far too complicated for easy summary. One must read it.

Yet anyone who has had much to do with previous Stein criticism reads Mr. Sutherland's first sentence with

46 *Ibid.*, xxvii.

a sinking heart: "This will be to explain as much as I understand of what Gertrude Stein did in writing."[47] It is the tone and cadence of Gertrude Stein herself when she is in her communicative mood; one thinks, she has found another creature. But one soon sees that this first impression is faulty: Mr. Sutherland is Gertrude Stein's man, but he is not her creature. Her writing is, of course, the raw material of his book, but he fits it into an independent aesthetic system that is his own structure, one with force and mass and cohesiveness. The structure is his own perforce, since her material had, pointedly, neither system nor structure—as Mr. Sutherland recognizes without misgiving. Reading further, we realize that Mr. Sutherland is among those who knew Miss Stein personally, but he avoids the trap of personality exploitation, just as he avoids every other trap, except illogic. His subtitle is exact: *A Biography of Her Work*, and he attends to the written word. Only once or twice does Mr. Sutherland make overt use of his acquaintance, as in this snapshot, which supplies interesting support for Thornton Wilder's description of the dynamic quality of Gertrude Stein's presence:

Anyone who ever met her must remember the direct innocence of her glance, how it flattered and appalled one at once by making one for the moment the most interesting thing in the world.[48]

[47] Donald Sutherland, *Gertrude Stein: A Biography of Her Work*, 1.
[48] *Ibid.*, 127.

All in all, Donald Sutherland's study is of such significance that anyone writing on Gertrude Stein, pro or con, will henceforth have to deal with it. He conducts his examination in six divisions, beginning with a chapter on "The Elements," which treats mainly Gertrude Stein's relationship to contemporary theories of consciousness, and closing with a chapter of "Meditations," a sequence of hypothetical questions and answers, gnomic and lively, nicely fantastic, and, if one attends closely, often illuminating. In the intervening chapters he proceeds, in a manner that is perhaps a shade too impressionistic to be thoroughly satisfying, through the list of Gertrude Stein's major productions in chronological order, spending most space, appropriately, on *Three Lives, The Making of Americans, Tender Buttons,* and the plays. Mr. Sutherland's chief lines of defense are arguments drawn in support of the aesthetic and artistic rightness of Gertrude Stein's attainment, as he sees it, of a series of highly original literary effects: the mating of language, rhythm, and character, the organicism as it were, of the early works; the stark freshness of insight in her abstract mode, in which the object is rendered as "unprejudiced and primitive experience,"[49] with a "direct sense of things as unique and unclassified";[50] the creation of a new literary time sense within the individual work, which Mr. Sutherland calls "legendary time."[51]

[49] *Ibid.,* 82.
[50] *Ibid.,* 74.
[51] *Ibid.,* 133.

Mr. Sutherland believes, quite rightly I think, that "the essential meaning of art in the first half of the 20th century" has been "the isolation and extrication of immediate quality from the whole unending complex of practical relations and associated substantives."[52] He assigns Miss Stein a very high place, perhaps the highest, higher than that of Proust or Joyce, in the pursuit of this literary ideal. Mr. Sutherland is convinced that she was one of the great seminal and symptomatic artists of this time, perhaps the one who had come closest of all to expressing its real genius. In this opinion he is simply seconding Gertrude Stein's own view of her position in contemporary letters: ". . . we who created the expression of the modern composition. . . ."[53] It is genuinely sad that Gertrude Stein could not have lived to see herself so ably expounded; Mr. Sutherland's book would have been one of the greatest pleasures of a career to which she always felt justice had never been done.

But Donald Sutherland can be exasperating, too, and occasionally absurd. He can commit such loose categoricals as ". . . no literature, once you are out of school and have heard everything, is interesting for what it has to say. Only for the way it is. . . ."[54] He is overfond of vague omnibus terms, especially "things": ". . . is an isolated thing and a disconnected thing our kind of thing?"[55] ". . .

[52] *Ibid.*, 177.
[53] Gertrude Stein, "Composition as Explanation," in *What Are Masterpieces*, 35–36.
[54] Sutherland, *op. cit.*, 118.
[55] *Ibid.*, 93.

an absolute and gratuitous thing in itself, as anything seems to want or like to be now."[56] There is an irritating tinge of snobbery in such a statement as ". . . one has to like freedom in order to like Gertrude Stein's work at all."[57] The statement is probably true, but one resents the implied sneer. Is Mr. Sutherland suggesting that those who do not like her work are probably enemies of freedom? Most displeasing and least justifiable of all Mr. Sutherland's habits is his tendency to specious comparison and false analogy. The following passage seems to me a cache of this kind of shabby reasoning:

> Tender Buttons *was intended to be available to anybody with a grade-school education, anybody who can count up to ten with confidence, add, subtract, and divide by two. The overt intellectual operations of* Tender Buttons *are no more complicated than that. Her use of parataxis and asyndeton, which is to say "and and and," or lists with no connection is simply counting. It is a child's way of counting or telling anything, and also the way of the* Iliad, *Hesiod, the Old Testament, and medieval litanies and prayers. Her constant use of* is *or* makes *as the main verb is a simple sum or equation. Again it is child's play, but the problem of one is three once split the world apart and the internal fission of the Trinity was as consequential as the fission of the atom.*[58]

[56] *Ibid.*, 99.
[57] *Ibid.*, 84.
[58] *Ibid.*, 95.

Throughout his study Mr. Sutherland is moved to place Gertrude Stein in company in which she simply does not belong. It is hard to believe that a man as intelligent as Donald Sutherland has been, as he says, enraptured by Miss Stein's writing; I cannot avoid the suspicion that it is once more the personality, rather than the writing, that has captured the disciple.

By the way of summary we can say of the body of criticism devoted to Gertrude Stein that it is a very curious one—and with a few exceptions, of which Mr. Sutherland's is the most marked, not particularly interesting. It is startlingly small, very generally mistaken, undernourished in fact, usually unbalanced in illogical admiration or in illogical peevishness, and characteristically low in specific gravity. What would Miss Stein say about all this? "No artist needs criticism, he only needs appreciation. If he needs criticism he is no artist."[59] Real art—that is, such as she was sure hers was—is by definition good and requires only admiration. In point of fact, Gertrude Stein behaved on the score of criticism just as we would expect anyone to behave. She craved critical recognition, preferred that it be "appreciation," but accepted any notice with forlorn pleasure. "They do quote me," she said. "That proves my sentences get under their skins."

What she really wanted, ironically enough, was readers. Now I must try to show why, as I see it, she had so few readers, so many samplers.

[59] Stein, *The Autobiography of Alice B. Toklas,* 194.

2

THE PARENT PROBLEM OF TIME:

The Complete Actual Present

The aesthetic theories of Gertrude Stein are intrinsically complex, and of course they are made vastly more difficult by the eccentricity of her phrasing. To approach her work with any hope of understanding it, we must go patiently by way of her stated intentions in art. We will find that these intentions center ultimately around her view of time and its importance to art and the artist—time variously defined, with many interrelated subdivisions. Gertrude Stein dwelt upon time to the point of fetishism. She was insistently and philosophically modern in seeing "contemporaneousness" as the supreme virtue in the arts. For the true creative artist, she believed, there is only one time, the present, and she measured success or failure in writing—hers and others'—by the degree to which the present is "realized" by the writer:

The business of Art . . . is to live in the actual present, that is the complete actual present, and to completely express that complete actual present.[1]

Three questions central to Gertrude Stein's writing and her aesthetics immediately present themselves. What is the "actual present" of her time? How does the artist apprehend it? How does he "completely express" it?

Miss Stein has documented her position on these questions throughout her writings, but most clearly in several essays that were delivered as lectures: "Composition As Explanation," 1926; "How Writing Is Written," 1935; and "What Are Masterpieces and Why Are There So Few of Them," 1935. In "Composition as Explanation," she concerns herself with precisely the problem of the artist's sense of his own time. By the "composition" of her title she means the things that "compose" the uniqueness of an era, the peculiarities of movement and vision that mark it off as a cultural entity from the period which preceded it and that will separate it from the one that follows. Miss Stein fits this difference into a framework of sameness; that is, she finds continuity in the broad outlines of history, but differentiation—peculiarly sharp in the twentieth century—in details of behavior. We find her generalization of the matter in these words:

Each period of living differs from any other period of

[1] Gertrude Stein, "Plays," in *Lectures in America,* 104–105.

living not in the way life is but in the way life is conducted and that authentically speaking is composition.[2]

Nothing changes from generation to generation except the thing seen and that makes a composition.[3]

The only thing that is different from one time to another is what is seen and what is seen depends upon how everybody is doing everything.[4]

What, then, is the "thing seen" that makes the "composition" of this generation? We should note first that Gertrude Stein uses the term "generation" loosely in the sense of a cultural time entity; for her a generation can occupy "anywhere from two years to a hundred years."[5] Thus she would date the twentieth century from the American Civil War and "the commercial conceptions that followed it."[6] This view of time leads Miss Stein to believe that the twentieth century is the "American century" and to hold the interesting corollary that America, having entered it first, is "now the oldest country in the world."[7] Then, in trying to define the "actual present" of the twentieth century, Miss Stein isolates as its distinguishing traits the physical facts of "the cinema and series pro-

[2] Stein, "Composition as Explanation," in *What Are Masterpieces,* 30.
[3] *Ibid.,* 26.
[4] *Ibid.,* 30.
[5] Gertrude Stein, "Portraits and Repetition," in *Lectures in America,* 165.
[6] Stein, *The Autobiography of Alice B. Toklas,* 65.
[7] *Ibid.*

duction"[8] and the metaphysical fact of a unique time sense developing from a unique intensity of movement.

The consequences of these factors, for her work at least, were vast, but one understands their implications better when one sees her actually at work; we should therefore pause now for a definition of only their general meanings to her. In the case of the cinema she was interested mainly in its technique of presentation by means of a blended succession of infinitesimally differentiated images. By contrast to the successive movement of the cinema, series production meant to her the twentieth-century technique of almost instantaneous creation, virtually eliminating a time factor, and the conception of a thing as a whole antecedent to a knowledge of its parts, the parts created, as it were, analytically or deductively from the whole. She puts the case this way:

> *The United States, instead of having the feeling of beginning at one end and ending at another, had the conception of assembling the whole thing out of its parts, the whole thing which made the Twentieth Century production. The Twentieth Century conceived an automobile as a whole, so to speak, and then created it, built it up out of its parts. It was an entirely different point of view from the Nineteenth Century's. The Nineteenth Century would have seen the parts, and worked towards the automobile through them.*[9]

[8] Stein, "Portraits and Repetition," in *Lectures in America,* 177.
[9] Gertrude Stein, "How Writing Is Written," in *The Oxford Anthology of American Literature* (ed. by William Rose Benét and Norman Holmes Pearson), II, 1447.

But the metaphysical element, the twentieth century's uniquely intense sense of movement, is at once more complex and more important for Miss Stein's work than are the cinema and series production. Because of it, finally, she turned her back upon narration as a possible procedure for a creative writer and moved definitively in the direction of still life and abstraction. If "the business of Art is . . . to express the complete actual present," and if it is true, as she says, that ". . . the Twentieth Century gives of itself a feeling of movement, and has in its way no feeling for events,"[10] then it is clear that the artist will record movement and not events: hence he will not write narrative in the conventional way.

Miss Stein's idea here is twofold and, I think, valid. First, by the internal intensity of movement in our time we have achieved a vitality that is self-animated and self-contained; by its intrinsic vigor this movement eliminates the necessity of a larger time context or perspective as a background against which to be perceived.[11] Second, by the very strength and multiplicity of events in our time, we have lost both the sense of orderly succession and the sense of the importance of the separate event:

The thing has got to this place, that events are so wonderful that they are not exciting. . . . I was struck with it during the war: the average doughboy standing on a street corner doing nothing . . . was much more exciting to peo-

[10] *Ibid.*, 1450.
[11] Stein, "Portraits and Repetition," in *Lectures in America*, 165–66.

ple than when the soldiers went over the top. . . . And it is a perfectly natural thing. Events had got so continuous that the fact that events were taking place no longer stimulated anybody . . . for our contemporary purposes, events have no importance . . . the kind of excitement the Nineteenth Century got out of events doesn't exist.[12]

The "actual present" of the twentieth century is colored, then, as that of any era is colored, by its peculiar time sense. The composition of a generation is the thing seen; the thing seen is the thing done; the things that are characteristically done in the twentieth century are the cinema and series production; to these are added the extreme intensity and multiplicity of movement and events. These are the forces that compose the tempo of our time, and they are, in outline, Gertrude Stein's answer to our first question concerning the nature of our "actual present."

As we have seen, the true artist for Miss Stein is the one who perceives his time as it is and records it fittingly. Our second question, how the artist is to manage this true perception, is harder to answer than our first. At one level, however, it is comparatively simple: one has merely to separate one's present from one's past. As Miss Stein put it in an address at the Choate School:

. . . everybody in his generation has his sense of time which belongs to his crowd. But then, you always have the mem-

[12] Stein, "How Writing Is Written," in *The Oxford Anthology of American Literature,* II, 1450.

ory of what you were brought up with. In most people that makes a double time, which makes confusion.[13]

She dramatized delightfully this incessant conflict of generations—one of the few times she consented to being dramatic at all—in the vignette that opens *The Making of Americans:*

Once an angry man dragged his father along the ground through his own orchard. "Stop!" cried the groaning old man at last, "Stop! I did not drag my father beyond this tree."[14]

Her principle here is a familiar one, and, as I have said, the resolution of this part of her problem is fairly simple: one can and does break away from one's parents. But for the few genuine creators, among whom she most emphatically numbers herself, the break is full of consequences, and these Miss Stein discusses with much eloquence and pathos. The break means, for one thing, that beauty is denied their work and, for another, that recognition and acclaim are denied them in their lifetime:

When one is beginning to write he is always under the shadow of the thing that is just past. And that is the reason why the creative person always has the appearance of ugliness . . . in struggling away from this thing there is always an ugliness.[15]

[13] *Ibid.*, 1448.
[14] Gertrude Stein, *The Making of Americans* (abridged ed.), 3.

This unavoidable ugliness of first creativity—a doctrine which, incidentally, she takes over whole from Picasso—constitutes one reason why the true artist is not recog-
37 nized by his contemporaries.

This failure of acceptance is further motivated by the gap between the sensitivity of the artist and that of Everyman. The artist and the layman are, of course, contemporary, but, as Thornton Wilder puts it in his preface to Miss Stein's *Narration*, "The artist is the most sensitive exponent of his contemporaneousness, expressing it while it still lies in the unconscious of society at large."[16] I should hasten to remark here that this is Wilder's phrasing and not Miss Stein's. She avoids Freudian terminology and, indeed, Freudian concepts with a stringency that casts some doubt on her own "contemporaneousness."

At any rate, the artist recognizes a truth that is hidden as yet from his fellows; consequently, his work is likely to seem to them both ugly and anachronistic. As a rule, public recognition of the truth of his vision waits for the next generation, which can accept the last generation's new vision as a thing with which their sense of their time has caught up, removing the conflict that blocked the artist's lagging contemporaries:

Those who are creating the modern composition authentically are naturally only of importance when they are dead

[15] Stein, "How Writing Is Written," in *The Oxford Anthology of American Literature*, II, 1448.

[16] Thornton Wilder, Preface to *Narration*, by Gertrude Stein, viii.

because by that time the modern composition having become past is classified and the description of it is classical. That is the reason why the creator of the new composition in the arts is an outlaw until he is a classic.[17]

Gertrude Stein was happy to be able to make an exception of her own time in this doleful pattern. There was a long period during which she feared she would die an outlaw, and even in 1935 she was still saying, "Thirty years from now I shall be accepted."[18] But because of the oddness of her period, its intensity of movement and consciousness, and the forced focusing of general awareness in a war that was itself abnormally "contemporary" in its knowledgeableness, she dared hope that she might instead die a classic:

And so the art creation of the contemporary composition which would have been outlawed normally outlawed several generations more behind even than war, war having been brought so to speak up to date art so to speak was allowed not completely to be up to date, but nearly up to date, in other words we who created the expression of the modern composition were to be recognized before we were dead some of us even quite a long time before we were dead. And so war may be said to have advanced a general recognition of the contemporary composition by almost thirty years.[19]

[17] Stein, "Composition as Explanation," in *What Are Masterpieces,* 27.
[18] Stein, "How Writing Is Written," in *The Oxford Anthology of American Literature,* II, 1447.

This statement impresses one as part truth, part *post hoc* rationalization—a feeling one has rather often in reading Miss Stein. At any rate, after the success of her *Autobiography of Alice B. Toklas, Four Saints in Three Acts,* and her American lecture tour of 1934–35, the fame that came to her was in some degree an embarrassment of riches. She seems to have been bothered by the feeling that this material success should not have happened to a true creator. Fame had, ironically, cast doubt on her genius, and in her *Everybody's Autobiography* of 1937 she does a good deal of twisting and turning in an amusing effort to reconcile fame and genius.

But to return to the main line of her argument: how is the artist to perceive his time? It will seem at first paradoxical to find Miss Stein saying, ". . . there is nothing that anyone creating anything needs more than that there is no time sense inside in them no past present or future."[20] The thing that really troubles her here, however, is the danger of a time sense at the moment of creation; hence the crucial phrase is "inside in them." Her position is clarified to some extent by another statement: ". . . for a genius time must not exist. . . . There must be a reality that has nothing to do with the passage of time."[21]

We are beginning to confront here what is probably the most fundamental problem in the implementa-

[19] Stein, "Composition as Explanation," in *What Are Masterpieces,* 35–36.
[20] Gertrude Stein, "An American and France," in *What Are Masterpieces,* 64–65.
[21] Gertrude Stein, *Everybody's Autobiography,* 154.

tion of Gertrude Stein's complex aesthetics. I should call it her doctrine of absolute creativity, her belief in the necessary uniqueness of the state of true creation. In views that one is tempted to call mystical, Miss Stein held that it is possible to "express the complete actual present"—for her the true function of art—only when one has maneuvered oneself into a condition above situation, a condition of selflessness and timelessness, and into a relation that we can call only oneness, or union of the artist and his subject. An appropriately cryptic rendering of the proposition occurs in this selection from *The Geographical History of America or the Relation of Human Nature to the Human Mind*:

> *The human mind writes what it is. . . . The human mind can write what it is because what it is is all that it is and as it is all that it is all it can do is to write.*[22]

The realization of this state of ideal creativity was her constant and passionate concern, and many passages in her writings testify to the poignancy of her struggle to attain it. In attempting to define it, she uses one of the most extensive of her many eccentric, specialized vocabularies—such terms as identity, entity, human nature, human mind, god, mammon, audience, and so on—terms that I shall try to translate as we encounter them in context. In the passage above, for example, by "the human mind,"

[22] Gertrude Stein, *The Geographical History of America or the Relation of Human Nature to the Human Mind*, 69.

Miss Stein means the specifically creative mind; by "what it is," she means that the subject and the perceiving mind having become effectively one thing, creation can therefore occur.

That this, too, is for Miss Stein predominantly a time problem becomes clear from such statements as this cardinal one from her essay, "The Gradual Making of The Making of Americans":

When I was up against the difficulty of putting down the complete conception I had of an individual . . . I was faced by the trouble that I had acquired all this knowledge gradually but when I had it I had it completely at one time . . . it was a terrible trouble to me. And a good deal of The Making of Americans was a struggle to do this thing, to make a whole present of something that it had taken a great deal of time to find out, but it was a whole there then within me and as such it had to be said.

That then and ever since has been a great deal of my work and it is that which has made me try so many ways to tell my story.[23]

The essence of the struggle, it is clear, is the making of a "whole present," by which Miss Stein means the making of a created thing that will shed its pastness absolutely, that will not only not seem to contain the pastness of the

[23] Gertrude Stein, "The Gradual Making of The Making of Americans," in *Selected Writings of Gertrude Stein* (hereafter referred to as *Selected Writings*), 218.

experience, but will actually not contain it insofar as she is capable of stripping it away in the experiencing and the writing; it will move instead in a state of constant, ongoing presentness.

All this is, of course, fearfully abstract, but it is also so basic in Miss Stein's aesthetics that one must come to grips with it. A logical approach can be made to this fearful abstraction through a tentative examination of Miss Stein's relationship to contemporary philosophy. The sources of the philosophical component of Miss Stein's work form one of the great unknowns about her, and the truth is very difficult to perceive. A few commentators have remarked her probable debt to modern philosophy, but there has been scarcely any exploration of the nature of the debt. William Troy, for example, notes that "before disposing of her work with any real comfort it is necessary to know a great deal . . . about William James and Bergson and Whitehead,"[24] but he pursues the matter no further. Dorothy Van Ghent assigns Miss Stein to Whitehead,[25] and Robert Haas assigns her to William James and Pragmatism.[26]

Against these views must be set the fact that she confesses no debt to any other thinker, that she makes no mention of any reading in modern philosophy, that she

[24] William Troy, "A Note on Gertrude Stein," *Nation*, Vol. CXXXVII (September 6, 1933), 274.

[25] Dorothy Van Ghent, "Gertrude Stein and the Solid World," in *American Stuff*, 218–22.

[26] Robert Haas, "Another Garland for Gertrude Stein," Introduction to *What Are Masterpieces*, by Gertrude Stein, 14–22.

invariably casts her thinking in language that is strictly her own. Her brother Leo's opinion, while it need not yet be taken as definitive, needs to be weighed. The relationship between this brother and sister will some day be the subject of an enormously interesting psychological study. The two "disaggregated," as Leo put it, about 1913, and his last letter to her expresses the "hope that we will all live happily ever after and maintain our respective and due proportions while sucking gleefully our respective oranges."[27] Apparently the separation was not bitter, but it was very positive; they never met again. Leo, from the loneliness and isolation in which he was maturing a first-rate aesthetics, watched the public flowering of his sister's art and ego, and in the books written toward the end of his life he commented on the phenomenon with amusement and dismay tempered by considerable sweetness. The sweetness, which seems genuine, does not alter the fact that his picture of Gertrude Stein is the most damning we have. On the score of her receptivity to philosophy, the thing that now concerns us, he remarks:

Gertrude had no interest whatever in science or philosophy and no critical interest in art or literature 'til the Paris period and, apart from college texts, never, in my time at least, read a book on these subjects. Her critical interest was entirely in character, in people's personalities. She was practically inaccessible to ideas.[28]

[27] Leo Stein, *Journey into the Self*, 57.
[28] *Ibid.*, 298.

Leo's opinion checks both with one's impression that her philosophical vocabulary is indigenous and with her failure to refer to readings in philosophy, but it does not account for the fact that she eventually evolved an aesthetic system that, for all its eccentricity and spectacular unevenness, remains genuinely coherent and in many ways impressive. By art, artifice, or accident, it had happened. And it is clearly true that her ignorance of philosophy was not so absolute as Leo implies. Her close association with both James and Whitehead is a matter of record. Much of her work at Radcliffe was under James's close direction, and he is said to have considered her his most brilliant woman pupil. The relationship with Whitehead was briefer, but intense: she and Miss Toklas were invited to spend a week end with the Whiteheads, but the beginning of World War I intervened, and they stayed six weeks. *The Autobiography of Alice B. Toklas* describes this period somewhat laconically: "Gertrude Stein and Doctor Whitehead walked endlessly around the country. They talked of philosophy and history."[29]

There can be no doubt, then, that Gertrude Stein was exposed to the thinking of these men. If we can trust the *Autobiography*—and there is always doubt on this score[30]—James was the stronger influence. "The really lasting impression of her Radcliffe life came through Wil-

[29] Stein, *The Autobiography of Alice B. Toklas*, 123.

[30] Cf., for example, Leo Stein, *op. cit.*, and Georges Braque, Eugene Jolas, Maria Jolas, Henri Matisse, André Salmon, and Tristan Tzara, "Testimony Against Gertrude Stein," Supplement to *transition*, Vol. XXIII (July, 1935).

liam James,"[31] she tells us, and it seems that her major philosophical preoccupations were already forming with the writing of her first book, *Three Lives*, some ten years before her meeting with Whitehead. But the real question is the degree to which such an idiosyncratic thinker as Gertrude Stein was capable of orderly assimilation of the ideas of any mind outside her own. One suspects privately that the result represents a loose amalgam of certain isolated theories of James and Whitehead and Miss Stein's modifications of them in the endless ruminations of many years. Her final position, with those antimoral and anti-intellectual aspects that I shall try to make slowly clear, would have been anathema to both men.

Ultimately, however, Miss Stein's divergences from her masters are more interesting and important than her kinship to them. For this reason, Robert Haas's essay, "Another Garland for Gertrude Stein," in which he develops her relationship to James and Pragmatism, is deceptive if taken as explanatory of her entire direction. Though oversimple in this sense, it can perform the service of illuminating a very important detail, our current problem of her theory of presentness.

It is certainly true, as Haas points out, that Gertrude Stein denies the monistic "block-universe" of the idealists, as does William James, and that she accepts the "pluriverse" of James as her reality. In the pluriverse of the Pragmatists, "reality is what you know it as."[32] The

[31] Stein, *The Autobiography of Alice B. Toklas*, 65.
[32] Horace M. Kallen, Introduction to *The Philosophy of William James*, by William James, 37.

supreme realities then become not the received absolutes of the idealists, but "time and change and chance"[33] as they are perceived by the individual from moment to moment. "All knowledge . . . is presently held, and . . . this present is in continual flux."[34] Pragmatism conceives as its "root-metaphor" the world "as an ongoing present event."[35] James himself upholds what he describes as "the manyness in oneness that indubitably characterizes the world we inhabit," the "through-and-through union of adjacent minima of experience, of the confluence of every passing moment of concretely felt experience with its immediately next neighbors."[36]

If we range alongside this "world of flux and presentness" of the Pragmatists such statements as Gertrude Stein's "A composition of a prolonged present is a natural composition in the world as it has been these last thirty years,"[37] it becomes clear that she is thinking in their manner. And if we return to her aesthetic credo as quoted earlier—to "begin again," as Miss Stein would say—"The business of Art . . . is to live in the actual present . . . and to completely express that complete actual present," we may easily agree with Mr. Haas that this is "the unmistakable definition of a pragmatic thinker."[38] Donald Sutherland recalls that Gertrude Stein was a student under Wil-

[33] Haas, *loc. cit.*, 15.
[34] *Ibid.*
[35] *Ibid.*, 17.
[36] William James, "The World We Live In," in *The Philosophy of William James*, 122.
[37] Stein, "Composition as Explanation," in *What Are Masterpieces*, 31.
[38] Haas, *loc. cit.*, 17.

liam James and Münsterberg at Radcliffe about 1895, at the time when there occurred the critical dispute concerning the nature of consciousness—whether it was an entity or a relation—which resulted in James's agreement with Bergson that consciousness was a relation, and his formulation, in consequence, of the system of Pragmatism and Radical Empiricism. But we cannot know, as Sutherland rightly says, whether Gertrude Stein absorbed her notion of "consciousness as thinking in relation"[39] directly from William James or whether her sense of the rightness of the view was merely coincidental with his. By coincidence, by direct acceptance, or by some combination, she had, at any rate, reached the position where "the idea that present thinking is the final reality was to be the axis or pole of Gertrude Stein's universe."[40] The question of whether Miss Stein's thinking here is specifically Jamesian, or is pragmatic in source, or comes from another source, or is indigenous to her is finally academic. The important thing to note is that somehow she had made her way into the main stream of contemporary philosophy, and probably of art as well, in her preoccupation with time and with thought process as reality. That she was so situated and that her position is important for her writing and thinking, this much we must accept. She would have been happy, at any rate, to see us witnessing the evidences of her modernity and "contemporaneousness" in being bothered by the complex interminglings of space and time. In

[39] Sutherland, *op. cit.*, 6.
[40] *Ibid.*, 7.

the twentieth century Miss Stein could have absorbed these ideas from the very air; and like a great many other "modern" philosophical concepts, the pragmatist view of time is as old as Heraclitus.

In realizing presentness, the duty of the artist is more complicated than mere keeping "up to date." For Miss Stein the matter is far more involved. The artist must not only "live in the actual present"; he must also "express" it; and in the expression comes the rub. We now approach the third general question I suggested at the beginning of this study. For Miss Stein the expression *itself* must be of an absolute presentness—a kind of perpetual "now"—hence the "terrible trouble . . . to make a whole present of something that it had taken a great deal of time to find out . . . which has made me try so many ways to tell my story."[41]

In a word, she seems to have been trying in her writing to transfix the "now" which, ironically, her master, James, had once described as "an altogether ideal abstraction, not only never realized in sense, but probably never even conceived of by those unaccustomed to philosophic meditation." It exists as "a sort of saddle-back of time with a certain length of its own, on which we sit perched, and from which we look in two directions into time."[42] Miss Stein's divergence from James, then, begins early, at the point where she begins to implement her theory.

[41] Stein, "The Gradual Making of The Making of Americans," in *Selected Writings*, 218.
[42] William James, *Psychology*, 280.

In the most characteristic portions of her work, she seems to attempt to disprove both parts of this proposition; she denies that the present is "never realized in sense," and that the genuinely creative artist, when perched on the "saddleback" of now, looks in "two directions into time" —a position that really resembles Whitehead's "specious present" with its penumbral shadings of past and future. Instead, the eye of the creative artist is fixed unswervingly on the present, traveling with it as it travels, refusing the enticements of both the past and the future. By disciplined meditation, Miss Stein believed, the artist can train himself to seize the present and move with it as if he were attached to the second hand of a watch, jumping as it jumps, into a new present. Thus the present reality becomes a finite thing, apprehensible and recordable.

Why is the present moment so important to her? Because it is the moment of perfect knowledge, of perfect union between the artist and his subject matter, when his object is what it *now* is, rather than what it was an instant ago. It is the moment, as it were, when reality is true. "Gertrude Stein," she tells us in her best Delphic style, ". . . has always been possessed by the intellectual passion for exactitude in the description of . . . reality."[43] For her, what is real is what is now real.

[43] Stein, *The Autobiography of Alice B. Toklas*, 174.

3

THE PARENT PROBLEM OF INTEGRITY:

Written Writing Should Not Be Led

Following the consequences to Gertrude Stein's aesthetics of her struggle for the "whole present" brings us to another major division of her thinking. It will clarify the matter at the outset if we turn to the conventional vocabulary of criticism, leaving Miss Stein's argot for the moment, and say that here she is primarily concerned with the integrity of the artist—how it may be realized and insured. Miss Stein uses many private equivalents for integrity—"human mind," "entity," "serving god," "one being completely talking and listening," "one being completely existing," and so on, but she means integrity nonetheless. The things to keep in mind are that integrity for her means the state of realization of true creativity and that this state is realized with the attainment of the magical moment of confluence and coexistence of artist, subject, and time. She calls this moment, in her simplest and most tangible descriptions, "the sense of the immediate"[1] and the state of "creative recognition."[2]

She found, she says, early in her career, that "there were two things I had to think about; the fact that knowledge is acquired, so to speak, by memory; but that when you know anything memory doesn't come in. At any moment that you are conscious of knowing anything, memory plays no part."[3] Once again the time problem emerges as fundamental. When we recall that the moment of knowledge must be the moment of creating and, further, that the moment of knowledge is confounded by the sense of a process of arriving at it—by memory—we see that memory, being of the past, is an enemy of the present and of creativity. Thus the literary artist must escape the past and its henchman, memory. Essentially it is a matter of separating true time from false time. To have integrity, to "serve god," to be a true creator, the artist must make this separation: ". . . I have been trying in every possible way to get the sense of immediacy, and practically all the work I have done has been in that direction."[4] Her dedication was sober and complete.

To make Miss Stein's researches in the integrity of absolute creativity at all clear, we shall have to stoop to considerable oversimplification. We can understand the

[1] Stein, "How Writing Is Written," in *The Oxford Anthology of American Literature,* II, 1448.
[2] John Hyde Preston, "A Conversation," *Atlantic Monthly,* Vol. CLVI (August, 1935), 188.
[3] Stein, "How Writing Is Written," in *The Oxford Anthology of American Literature,* II, 1448.
[4] *Ibid.,* 1449.

thing best if we divide it into its two main problems, which she calls "identity" and "audience." This division is oversimple in that these concepts are by no means the whole of the parent problem and in that they are not really separable, any more than any two portions of her aesthetic thought are separable. For her aesthetics—in spite of its seeming abstruseness and linguistic incoherence—is logically coherent. In explicating these more fugitive and recherché areas of her thinking, it will no longer be possible to avoid some of her more spectacular prose; it is, after all, high time that the reader suffer a bit with the writer.

We can at least begin simply, by borrowing a brief synopsis from Thornton Wilder, who alone among Gertrude Stein's commentators recognizes the importance of the concepts of identity and audience for her aesthetic theory. Mr. Wilder treats the matter briefly in his introduction to *The Geographical History of America or the Relation of Human Nature to the Human Mind* and at greater length in the impressive essay introducing Miss Stein's posthumous *Four in America.* In reading Wilder's summary, one should recall that Miss Stein used the term "human mind" as an equivalent of the genuinely creative mind and the term "human nature" as an equivalent of the mind barred from creativity by the burden of possessing the sense of identity and audience, among, of course, other burdens:

Human Nature clings to identity, its insistence on itself as personality, and to do this it must employ memory and the sense of an audience. By memory it is reassured of its existence through consciousness of itself in time-succession. By an audience it is reassured of itself through its effect on another. . . . The Human Mind, however, has no identity. . . . It gazes at pure existing. It is deflected by no consideration of an audience, for when it is aware of an audience it has ceased to "know."[5]

Identity, then, in Wilder's perfectly accurate formulation, is the sin of the uncreative self, insisting on personality and employing memory to "reassure" itself of existence in time. To turn to Gertrude Stein's own phrasing:

There are so few masterpieces because mostly people live in identity and memory that is when they think. They know they are they because their little dog knows them, and so they are not an entity but an identity. And being so memory is necessary to make them exist and so they cannot create master-pieces.[6]

Miss Stein borrows the phrase "I am I because my little dog knows me" from a nursery rhyme as her private symbol for all those definings of the self that are dependent on past experience and remembering. The phrase becomes a kind of leitmotiv in *The Geographical History of America,* Miss Stein's fullest and most difficult treatment

[5] Thornton Wilder, Introduction to *The Geographical History of America,* by Gertrude Stein, 7–8.
[6] Gertrude Stein, "What Are Masterpieces and Why Are There So Few of Them," in *What Are Masterpieces,* 90.

of the problems of identity and audience. In that book we are told, "There is no remembering and no forgetting because memory has to do with human nature and not with the human mind";[7] that ". . . identity has nothing whatever to do with the human mind";[8] and that ". . . the human mind does not remember it knows and it writes what it knows."[9]

Now, lest we forget that we are dealing essentially with a time problem and that we are still in search of the "whole present," we should observe that "the human mind has to say what anything is now . . . oh yes yes yes that is the human mind."[10] We are still in touch with the time problem as well, in the sense of the artist's duty of realizing his "contemporaneousness," the "composition" of his own era's actual present, for Miss Stein finds our time peculiarly inhospitable to remembering:

We in this period have not lived in remembering, we have lived in moving being necessarily so intense that existing is indeed something, is indeed that thing we are doing.[11]

The true artist will recognize, then, not "remembering," but the "intensity" of the "existing" as our characteristic "composition."

Miss Stein returns us at last to the original dilem-

[7] Stein, *The Geographical History of America*, 81.
[8] *Ibid.*, 107.
[9] *Ibid.*, 111.
[10] *Ibid.*, 137.
[11] Stein, "Portraits and Repetition," in *Lectures in America*, 182.

ma, adumbrated in "The Gradual Making of The Making of Americans"—how to record the present knowing:

I kept wondering as I talked and listened all at once, I wondered is there any way of making what I know come out as I know it, come out not as remembering.[12]

In elucidating the specific "audience" portion of the problem, Thornton Wilder, who was long a sympathetic, if frequently bewildered, friend of Gertrude Stein, is again helpful:

It has often seemed to me that Miss Stein was engaged in a series of spiritual exercises whose aim was to eliminate during the hours of writing all those whispers into the ear from the outside and inside world where audience dwells.[13]

"Audience," to define the term as simply as possible, means "the sense in the writer of writing for a reader." Audience is intimately bound up with identity, and Miss Stein saw the two as the supreme enemies of genuine creation. "I am I because my little dog knows me" shows the mingling of audience and identity. She means here that the writer is conscious of himself as a self when he becomes aware that he is making an effect upon another.

Later Miss Stein carried this concern to the logical

[12] *Ibid.*, 181.
[13] Wilder, Introduction to *Four in America*, by Gertrude Stein, xiii.

extreme of troubling herself not only about the external audience, but also about the fact that the writer can be an audience to himself, again becoming guilty of audience and identity by, as it were, self-consciousness of self. Why bother? Simply because in the true creative act there must be no self: the self must have merged with the subject and the moment of knowledge; it is like Marvell's and Eliot's rolling the universe into one ball and spinning with it through time.

At last, in *Four in America,* she can exclaim happily, "I am I not any longer when I see."[14] And, she assures us, "This sentence is at the bottom of all creative activity. It is just the exact opposite of I am I because my little dog knows me."[15] To elucidate: "I am not I"—I am truly creative—"when I see," when I am drowned in the moment of knowing my subject.

Clearly, anyone attempting an evaluation of Gertrude Stein must take the concept of audience heavily into account, for in a studied philosophical act she denies that the artist can be conscious of any recipient of his work. The perfect artist creates *in vacuo,* and if his work finds an ear, it is by an act of God—not really to be expected in the order of things. She would claim, of course, that when providentially the work finds an audience, that audience will be enriched by the unique truth of the work created in obliviousness to an audience. Although this is by no means a new idea, it is highly impressive as a theory

[14] Gertrude Stein, "Henry James," in *Four in America,* 119.
[15] *Ibid.*

and an ideal, for it contains a great deal of truth. However, several things need to be pointed out here. For one thing, if the theory is to be productive of good art, the artist must be a good artist to begin with. For another, like most absolutes, the theory requires some modification to become practicable, and this qualification Gertrude Stein was never willing to allow. Instead, she pursued a course that excluded audience absolutely, thereby demanding a progressively more stringent concentration upon the sensorium of the artist alone. If this process is entirely unrelieved, it leads ultimately to a self-canceling private art. Inability to see this truism constituted Miss Stein's fatal blind spot; it amounted, finally, to something very near schizophrenia. Gertrude Stein's art is finally private and self-canceling, and it seems to me that it is therefore not art. But such judgments need to be slowly validated.

None of this is to say that Miss Stein did not care whether or not she was read. She wanted passionately to be read, and many eloquent passages in her writings testify to her hope that her work, after creation, would find the vast audience she felt it eminently deserved. Her attitude represents in a measure, once more, her tremendous ego and her near-schizophrenic inability to distinguish between the ideal and the real. "I always wanted to be historical, from almost a baby on,"[16] she tells us. And this passage from *The Making of Americans* is heavy with her early despair of finding readers:

[16] Gertrude Stein, "A Message from Gertrude Stein," in *Selected Writings*, vii.

Bear it in your mind my reader, but truly I never feel it that there ever can be for me any such a creature, no it is this scribbled and dirty and lined paper that is to be to me always my receiver.[17]

Everybody's Autobiography is full of her delight in the applause that followed the publication of *The Autobiography of Alice B. Toklas* and her lecture tour of America in 1934–35. In the latter book, the one that really made her famous, she says, "Not . . . that she could ever have enough of glory."[18] But her joy was clouded by the knowledge that glory was coming as a consequence of her least characteristic, in her own eyes least "creative," works, and as a consequence of the force of her personality—not from the art to which she had really devoted her life. Gertrude Stein could never understand or reconcile herself to the fact that her private, idiosyncratic art would inevitably find its way into cult and coterie. With a very genuine, if blind, bewilderment she says, "It has always been rather ridiculous that she who is good friends with all the world and can know them and they can know her, has always been the admired of the precious."[19] Ironically, she wanted readers, not collectors.

But to return to her development of the theory of audience itself. In an early, weak moment Gertrude Stein wrote, "I write for myself and strangers."[20] Ideally, of

[17] Stein, *The Making of Americans*, 37.
[18] Stein, *The Autobiography of Alice B. Toklas*, 194.
[19] *Ibid.*, 59.
[20] Stein, *The Making of Americans*, 211.

course, one should write neither for oneself nor for strangers, for both are audience. In a later lecture she caught up this passage, denounced it, and established what was for her the true position:

> *. . . that was merely a literary formalism for if I did write for myself and strangers if I did I would not really be writing because already then identity would take the place of entity.*[21]

To recall again the connection between audience and identity, the essential pastness of both and their mingling as enemies of true creation, we may cite this passage from *The Geographical History of America:*

> *Now identity remembers and so it has an audience and as it has an audience it is history and as it is history it has nothing to do with the human mind.*[22]

But the crux of the matter may be better dug out of a more cryptic passage, such as the following: "Written writing should not be led oh no it should not be led not at all led."[23] By "led" Miss Stein means here led or directed by the consciousness in the writer of the need of pleasing or conciliating an auditor, an awareness which, of course, is fatal to art.

[21] Stein, "What Are Masterpieces," in *What Are Masterpieces,* 86.
[22] Stein, *The Geographical History of America,* 111.
[23] *Ibid.,* 181.

Probably the most interesting of Miss Stein's approaches to the theory of audience is her lecture, "What Is English Literature." In it one learns, unfortunately, very little about English literature, but a great deal about Miss Stein's ideas on literary integrity. She discusses the conflict between "serving god" and "serving mammon," but it is the same old problem of audience in different terms. With "serving god" Miss Stein would equate "entity" and "human mind"; with "serving mammon," "identity" and "human nature." Here she makes her view fairly clear:

> *When I say god and mammon concerning the writer writing, I mean that anyone can use words to say something. And in using these words to say what he has to say he may use those words directly or indirectly. If he uses these words indirectly he says what he intends to have heard by somebody who is to hear and in so doing inevitably he has to serve mammon. Mammon may be a success, mammon may be an effort he is to produce, mammon may be a pleasure he has from hearing what he himself has done, mammon may be his way of explaining, mammon may be a laziness that needs nothing but going on, in short mammon may be anything that is done indirectly. Now serving god for a writer who is writing is writing anything directly, it makes no difference what is is but it must be direct. . . . slowly you will see what I mean. If not why not.*[24]

[24] Gertrude Stein, "What Is English Literature," in *Lectures in America,* 23–24.

To sample her more difficult expository manner we may try this passage from the same essay:

61 *In the nineteenth century what they thought was not what they said, but they said what they thought and they were thinking about what they thought. . . .*[25]

As I say in the nineteenth century what they thought was not what they said, but and this may sound like the same thing only it is not, they said what they thought and they were thinking about what they thought. This made the nineteenth century what it was.[26]

To translate, nineteenth-century writers recorded not their knowing as it was at the moment of knowing—pure—but their knowing as they knew it in reflecting on how they wanted to have it heard—adulterated. The nineteenth century served mammon, then, and committed the sins of identity, memory, audience, and human nature.

The time factor enters the theory of audience in another interesting way. Miss Stein saw that the conditioned reader would expect to find the kind of thing he had read. The alert writer, with integrity, recognized that in defeating this conditioned, expectant reader, he at once removed one of the attractions of audience and forced upon himself modernity or "contemporaneousness." In keeping ahead of the expectations of the reader —beyond the outposts of his experience—the writer is driven constantly to new designs in form and treatment:

[25] *Ibid.*, 39–40. [26] *Ibid.*, 40–41.

The writer is to serve god or mammon by writing the way it has been written or by writing the way it is being written that is to say the way writing is writing. . . . If you write the way it has already been written . . . then you are serving mammon.[27]

She puts it more conventionally and therefore more clearly in her lecture at the Choate School. We are reduced to being grateful that in this lecture, Miss Stein relaxed her battle with audience for the moment to let herself be aware that she was talking to boys, for this is probably the most intelligible of the summary reflections of her aesthetic position. Here is her most succinct analysis of the time essence of "audience":

If he doesn't put down the contemporary thing, he isn't a great writer, for he has to live in the past. . . . The minor poets of the period, or the precious poets of the period, are all people who are under the shadow of the past. A man who is making a revolution has to be contemporary. A minor person can live in the imagination.[28]

"A minor person can live in the imagination" makes the important new point that modernity must be present both in subject matter and in technique. By this sentence we are now led into the hinterlands of Gertrude

[27] *Ibid.*, 54.
[28] Stein, "How Writing Is Written," in *The Oxford Anthology of American Literature*, II, 1450.

Stein's researches into pure creativity. This, too, is an area we shall have to traverse. A whole host of problem children, spawned by the parent problem of absolute cre-
63 ativity, now stand up to be counted, but by grouping and compressing, it is possible to master the more important of them. Because they are all concepts of weight in Miss Stein's thinking and writing, all must be accounted for.

4

PROPER AND IMPROPER SUBJECT MATTER:

Time and Identity Is What You Tell About

The truth is that in examining those procedures that for her were not pure creativity, Gertrude Stein denounces most of what we are accustomed to consider the "proper" matter and manner of art. Kenneth Burke, in writing of what he sees as Miss Stein's preoccupation with form at the expense of subject matter, says that she is attempting to achieve an "art by subtraction."[1] The phrase is pithy and much more broadly applicable than Mr. Burke makes it in his essay. In a very real sense, subtraction in the field of the arts is her most characteristic activity. She dismisses and strips away the traditional until all that is left, finally, is her own very personal, very narrow art—the thin result of a complex and frequently impressive aesthetics.

In order to clarify these ramified corollary portions

[1] Burke, "Engineering With Words," *Dial*, Vol. LXXIV (April, 1923), 410.

of Miss Stein's aesthetics, I will subsume them under the headings of "matter" and "manner," and attempt to answer the questions of what is proper and improper subject matter, what is proper and improper technique for the genuine creative artist. At once we have to "begin again" with Miss Stein, recalling one of the capital statements of her creed:

> *Gertrude Stein . . . has always been possessed by the intellectual passion for exactitude in the description of inner and outer reality. She has produced a simplification by this concentration, and as a result the destruction of associational emotion in poetry and prose. She knows that beauty, music, decoration, the result of emotion should never be the cause, even events should not be the cause of emotion nor should they be the material of poetry and prose. Nor should emotion itself be the cause of poetry and prose. They should consist of an exact reproduction of either an inner or an outer reality.*[2]

When we add to these sweeping dismissals the whole vast area of the "imagination," which Gertrude Stein has already allocated to "minor" or "precious" writers, and reflect abruptly that we have catalogued here virtually all that centuries of writers have taught us is their real province, the full iconoclasm of her thinking becomes quickly apparent.

We are told, too, that we would have been mis-

[2] Stein, *The Autobiography of Alice B. Toklas*, 174.

taken to assume, as we might well have been tempted, that Miss Stein's definition of the creative state is Plato's "ecstasy" of creation with its fringe of madness. Hers is a far soberer thing; its main components are *gravitas* and absence of passion. "Exact reproduction" is her end, and her means begins with the subtraction of that extraneousness in which other writers have found their content. What we have here is something very close to the so-called "reduction" process of the Phenomenologists, and one cannot help wondering whether Miss Stein had encountered Husserl or his followers. I am inclined to suspect that this process, too, goes back to her association with William James, but to James as psychologist rather than as philosopher. It was, after all, at the psychological-laboratory level that she knew James most intimately, and one may conclude, uncharitably but justly, that the important thing Gertrude Stein took away from that association was not the philosophical large-mindedness, the broad humaneness of James, but the much narrower and more bloodless ideal of scientific "objectivity." If this impression is as sound as it seems, it helps to explain a great deal of Gertrude Stein's direction. It is almost as if she had taken James' injunction to "keep your mind open"[3] as the whole of the man and assumed that the mind is never to be allowed to close upon a truth. She leaves James at this point and retreats into a barren cavern of her own making; it is surgically clean and hospitable to objectivity, but there is not much life there.

[3] *Ibid.*, 67.

At any rate, the passage seems to give us a fairly complete summary answer to our questions. Along with imagination, Miss Stein lists beauty, music, decoration, events, and emotion as improper subject matter; proper subject matter is "inner and outer reality." Beauty, music, and decoration have no place in the artist's proper technique; proper technique consists of "description" or "reproduction"—the latter is closer to her final position—of proper subject matter, and it will proceed by "simplification" and "concentration" toward the "destruction of associational emotion." This much is clear. But the connotations of these terms for her and the route by which she arrived at this position need a good deal of tracing and amplification for sharp definition.

With this goal in mind, we should remind ourselves of the primacy of the time problem by recalling other dicta of Gertrude Stein:

The business of Art . . . is to live in . . . and to completely express . . . the complete actual present.[4]

. . . the human mind knows what it knows and knowing what it knows it has nothing to do with seeing what it remembers.[5]

Master-pieces . . . are knowing that there is no identity and producing while identity is not.[6]

[4] Stein, "Plays," in *Lectures in America*, 104–105.
[5] Stein, *The Geographical History of America*, 27.
[6] Stein, "What Are Masterpieces," in *What Are Masterpieces*, 90–91.

These statements, it will be readily seen, are central to Miss Stein's notion of the true creative state: a condition of almost mystical union of subject-artist-time in one magical bundle of "knowing." One thinks of such terms as *Aufklärung,* or even of the principle of "epiphany" in the early Joyce; but the added element of time, in the form of the necessary ongoing presentness of the "knowing," makes it less a bundle than a rolling ball of knowing, and our earlier metaphor is finally more satisfying.

On the basis of these dicta, we can logically conjecture that "beauty, music, decoration, events, emotion" are unwelcome to Gertrude Stein because they conflict with the ideal creative state. Indeed, this is the case; in various ways, as she sees it, they do conflict, and they must be cast into hell-fire. Although her attitude is thus sweepingly iconoclastic, it is at least all of a piece, part of a single coherent body of thought. Most of our conventional subject materials are herded together and damned by Miss Stein for the cardinal sins of pastness—remembering and identity—thereby cutting off the mind laboring to create from the ideal presentness of knowledge and forcing upon it the consciousness of the historical process of its knowing and hence the fatal consciousness of self.

From one point of view, however, "events" are improper subject matter in a somewhat different sense, and we can isolate that aspect for separate treatment. Events, as noted earlier, are improper matter because they are anachronistic; they are not part of the true "composition" of our time: "To the Twentieth Century events are not important."[7] This conviction led Miss Stein into some very curious attitudes, into some of those frequent specious, perverse opinions that so sadly mar the total picture of her aesthetics and make it so difficult to weigh. On this basis she was able, for example, to rationalize a great admiration for the detective story as "the only really modern novel form . . . the hero is dead to begin with and so you have so to speak got rid of the event before the book begins."[8] She was even moved to attempt the genre herself, although the result, *Blood on the Dining Room Floor*, resembles the conventional detective story only in its title.

At any rate, the consequences of removing events from the possible subject matter of a writer are clear: he cannot deal with happenings, with a course of events put together along a story line in the way that makes up what we usually call plot. It is significant that only the three earliest of Miss Stein's "creative" books, *Three Lives, The Making of Americans*, and the "forgotten" first novel, posthumously published as *Things as They Are*, contain a recognizable story line, and in *The Making of Americans*, it is merely rudimentary. She justifies this exclusion on the grounds of the anachronism of narrative and blows it up into a trend in which she is among the great figures:

. . . in the three novels written in this generation that are the important things written in this generation, there is,

[7] Stein, "How Writing Is Written," in *The Oxford Anthology of American Literature*, II, 1450.

[8] Stein, "What Are Masterpieces," in *What Are Masterpieces*, 87.

in none of them a story. There is none in Proust in The Making of Americans or in Ulysses.[9]

This, however, is another of her half-truths. Many writers, enough to constitute a major trend, have felt that a narrative method is not consonant with the subtler, more ramified "knowledge" of ourselves gained from twentieth-century science and psychology, and have therefore modified or suppressed the classical narrative line. But all, even Joyce, have retained enough rudiments of narrative to keep us roughly posted in space and time; it simply is not true that there is "no" story in Proust or even the Joyce of *Finnegans Wake*. Gertrude Stein, on the other hand, has sought obliteration of the narrative line, and her work, on these grounds as well as others, is not strictly comparable to anything in the main stream of literature in our century.

Events, in addition to committing the private sin of anachronism, share in what is for Miss Stein a deadlier sin, that of forcing memory and identity upon the writer:

I wrote a story as a story, that is the way I began, and slowly I realized this confusion, a real confusion, that in writing a story one had to be remembering. . . . It is this element of remembering that makes novels so soothing. But and that was the thing I was gradually finding out . . . realizing the existence of living being actually existing did not have in it any element of remembering and so the time

[9] Stein, "Portraits and Repetition," in *Lectures in America*, 184.

of existing was not the same as in the novels that were soothing.[10]

Here, "realizing the existence of living being actually existing" represents another of Miss Stein's synonyms for the familiar concept of the ongoing present knowledge, the pragmatist reality.

"Nor should emotion itself be the cause of poetry or prose," says Gertrude Stein, and the flaw in emotion, as in events, is that emotion contributes to identity and consciousness of self:

The pleasures that are soothing all have to do with identity and the pleasures that are exciting all have to do with identity and moreover there is all the pride and vanity which play about master-pieces . . . and these too all have to do with identity.[11]

To make the picture absolute: "The human mind has nothing to do with sorrow and with disappointment and with tears."[12]

On the topic of sex as subject matter Miss Stein gives a very curious performance indeed. At one point she writes that "sex and jealousy is not the human mind"[13] and are therefore improper matter, but in another context she reverses herself categorically; John Hyde Preston

[10] *Ibid.*, 181.
[11] Stein, "What Are Masterpieces," in "*What Are Masterpieces*, 91.
[12] Stein, *The Geographical History of America*, 31.
[13] *Ibid.*, 67.

quotes her as saying to him: "Sex and death are the springs of the most valid of human emotions . . . creative literature unconcerned with sex is inconceivable."[14] Whatever her true opinion, the absence of a sexual element is one of the inescapable impressions one takes from her writings. If it is there, it is so successfully sublimated that it is nowhere visible. At least one could say this until the publication in 1950 of *Things as They Are,* a book with a curious history. It was Gertrude Stein's first work of any length, but apparently she never wanted to publish it. She says in *The Autobiography of Alice B. Toklas* that she put the manuscript in a drawer after finishing it and "forgot" it until she came across it by chance in later life. But Gertrude Stein was not one to withhold anything publishable without very good reason, and one doubts the story of her forgetfulness in this case. Eventually, at any rate, the manuscript came into the possession of Carl Van Vechten, and he authorized its publication four years after Miss Stein died.

Things as They Are is sexual with a vengeance. It presents the young Gertrude Stein, transparently disguised as Adele (to whom she applies the epithets she liked to apply to herself—"impetuous and slow-minded,"[15] "commonplace and middle-class,"[16] full of "inertia"), coquetting about the fringes of an established Lesbian relationship between two other "college bred American women of

[14] Preston, "A Conversation," *Atlantic Monthly,* Vol. CLVI (August, 1935), 191.
[15] Gertrude Stein, *Things as They Are,* 30.
[16] *Ibid.,* 6.

the wealthier class,"[17] Helen and Sophie. Adele's performance in this affair, like that of Gertrude Stein the writer on sex, is strange and equivocal. There is nothing equivocal about the Lesbian attachment between Helen and Sophie, however. As far as one can tell, Adele never quite takes the complete plunge. There are "kisses" and "passionate embraces," but for Adele they seem to be mainly exploratory, tentative and still basically maidenly dippings into an area of life that both fascinates and repels her. Adele as a lover is dilettante and perverse. As Helen says to her:

> . . . *after all you haven't a nature much above passionettes. You are so afraid of losing your moral sense that you are not willing to take it through anything more dangerous than a mudpuddle.*[18]

Adele's virginal and intellectualized flirting becomes rather tedious to the reader, and to the other principals it must have been trying in the extreme. She seems to have had little real feeling for either of the other girls and to have used their more genuine passions ultimately only as touchstones for the trying out of her own fundamentally Puritan "morality" and her rather low-keyed "instincts." The book conveys little more at last than that Adele was incapable of complete commitment, although capable of tentative, intermittent, usually delayed response. At the end one is bored with Adele because of her indecisiveness

[17] *Ibid.*, 4.
[18] *Ibid.*, 12.

and the blithe way in which she complicates and saddens an already tense relationship.

Although it is hard to believe that Gertrude Stein did not have some such experience as that of Adele—the book is tinged with that degree of intimacy which always suggests autobiographical sources—one cannot, of course, impugn her sexuality. Dark suspicions are certainly possible, but I am more inclined to attribute her literary attitude toward sex to that pathological ability to compartmentalize her mind that I have called near schizophrenic. For some reason, to be sure, overt sex was distasteful to Gertrude Stein, seemingly in both life and literature. Bravig Imbs, for example, could attribute his fall from grace in the Stein salon only to the fact that he had discussed the pregnancy of his wife with Miss Stein and Miss Toklas.[19] She impressed W. G. Rogers, significantly, as "a kind of dynamic neuter . . . no more carnal than a portly abbot."[20] Finding sex distasteful, she ignored it, and then, by a manipulation of a very manageable mind and conscience, convinced herself that she had written "creative literature concerned with sex." In this way she was able to comfort her vagaries of sensibility and to retain undamaged her conviction of her "contemporaneousness."

There are a good many subjects other than events and emotion which Miss Stein does not mention in her statement of creed, but which she denounces emphatically in other portions of her writing. In this process she grad-

19 Bravig Imbs, *Confessions of Another Young Man*, 216.
20 W. G. Rogers, *When This You See Remember Me*, 43.

ually fills out an attitude one can only call sweepingly antimoral and anti-intellectual. Thus the true creator, she insists, cannot concern himself with "causes," with moral distinctions of right and wrong, with learning, with meanings, or with relationships or generalizations or problems of cause and effect. Although her statement of these opinions is often fragmentary and unclear, one must not think that she held them any the less strongly.

Her unconcern with the things we have loosely called "causes" is shown, for example, in *The Geographical History of America:* ". . . the writing that is the human mind does not consist in messages."[21] Less esoterically, she tells a friend from college days that she "does not at all mind the cause of women or any other cause but it does not happen to be her business."[22] It is not difficult to see the tremendous reaches of passionate human concern here quarantined by an arbitrary act. Gertrude Stein's most characteristic gesture, subtraction, continues to work.

Her private brand of realism enjoins her also to remain aloof to meanings in the phenomena she observes. "Anything that is," she says, "is quite enough if it is";[23] again, "The minute it means anything it is not concerned with the human mind."[24] The artist, with his "intellectual passion for exactitude in the description of reality," is barred by the absoluteness of that preoccupation from reflecting upon the implications of his experience. Its im-

[21] Stein, *The Geographical History of America,* 80.
[22] Stein, *The Autobiography of Alice B. Toklas,* 69.
[23] Stein, *Everybody's Autobiography,* 6.
[24] Stein, *The Geographical History of America,* 54.

plications are no part of his "business." That this tendency is extensible to specifically moral problems is also clear, for "... the human mind ... is not concerned with being or not being true."[25] One begins to harbor the nasty suspicion that Gertrude Stein, whether she knows it or not, is really involved in a colossally elaborated, intricately rationalized process of evasion, which is likely to lead, finally, to an arrant escape literature.

The full antimorality and anti-intellectualism of her position are made abundantly clear in the following passage, which serves also to remind us that we are still entirely under the discipline of the parent problems of time and creativity:

It is only in history government, propaganda that it is of any importance if anybody is right about anything. Science well they never are right about anything not right enough so that science cannot go on enjoying itself as if it is interesting, which it is. . . . Master-pieces have always known that being right would not be anything because if they were right then it would be not as they wrote but as they thought and in a real master-piece there is no thought, if there were thought then there would be that they are right and in a master-piece you cannot be right, if you could it would be what you thought not what you do write.

Write and right.

Of course they have nothing to do with one another.

[25] *Ibid.*, 110.

Right right left right left he had a good job and he left, left right left.[26]

77 To bring the matter back to the real problem of the description of "reality":

As I say it makes no difference because although I am always right is being right anything . . . there is something so much more pleasing and that is what is what. And what is what is what is what.[27]

Gertrude Stein's eyes-fixed concentration on the present "reality" has a further, very serious consequence that is yet another facet of her anti-intellectualism. She rejects, because of its inevitable dependence on the past and hence its tendency to rely on memory and identity, man's very faculty for learning, for absorbing intellectually the data of his senses, ordering them into relationships, generalizing upon them, and advancing thereby to new intellectual frontiers—the faculty, in a word, that we have always fondly believed separated us from the lower animals. These capacities, being rooted in the past, have no validity for the true creator. "What is the use of being a little boy," Miss Stein asks pungently, "if you are going to grow up to be a man?"[28] She develops the aphorism further in "What Are Masterpieces":

[26] *Ibid.*, 198–99.
[27] *Ibid.*, 201–202.
[28] *Ibid.*, 22.

. . . the boy and the man have nothing to do with each other, except in respect to memory and identity, and if they have anything to do with each other in respect to memory and identity then they will never produce a master-piece.[29]

But we are not yet done with the matter, and we should not leave Miss Stein's anti-intellectualism without noting the full preciosity, the distastefully hermetic quality of her position. We find her saying:

. . . the master-piece has to do with the human mind and the entity that is with a thing in itself and not in relation. The moment it is in relation it is common knowledge and anybody can know it and it is not a master-piece . . . master-pieces exist because they came to be as something that is an end in itself and in that respect it is opposed to the business of living which is relation and necessity.[30]

Real art, then, is opposed to the business of living, and a realist, a pragmatic thinker, has made a curious progress. James and Whitehead have taken leave of her long ago.

To be absolutely fair to Miss Stein, we must remark that her enmity is clearly not directed toward learning per se or toward learning as a respectable activity of the human animal. She would insist merely, with her aptitude for schizophrenic separations, that it is a cate-

29 Stein, "What Are Masterpieces," in *What Are Masterpieces*, 90.
30 *Ibid.*, 88.

gory of the mind insulated from the mind's creative compartment—and inferior to it.

A kind of primitivism certainly reveals itself in Miss Stein's desire to keep the artist a perpetual naïf. If she were advocating primitivism alone, her position would be easier to respect, but she has refined upon primitivism and added to it something very old and very tired: art-for-art. The view that art and the artist himself are the final repositories of value is the inevitable outcome of Miss Stein's "something that is an end in itself . . . opposed to the business of living."

In surveying Miss Stein's theory of improper subject matter, I have shown that her art by subtraction has subtracted imagination, events, emotion, "causes," "meanings," moral distinctions, and learning in its elements of generalization, relationships, and logical causation. What is left, one asks, as the artist's proper matter? Pitifully little, one may well fear. In exploring this poverty, we will find ourselves involved in at least seeming paradox on the one hand and in extreme abstraction on the other, for this is one of Gertrude Stein's ultimate lairs; trapped within it, she uses her ultimate weapons of defense.

We can point up both the paradox and the abstraction, and at the same time their essential oneness, with a single brief quotation from Miss Stein: "And yet time and identity is what you tell about as you create only while you create they do not exist."[31]

The paradox lies in the fact that the artist's im-

[31] *Ibid.*, 92.

proper subject matter is at the same time his inevitable subject matter. "Time and identity is what you tell about"; that is, all those things that make you know time and identity—emotion, events, learning, and so on—are your inevitable subject matter. The abstraction enters in the artist's effort to insure that "while you create they do not exist." To achieve this end the artist must disguise his subject, not only from the reader, but more importantly from himself. But patently obliviousness to subject matter is not possible as long as vestiges of its "time and identity" remain; to disguise it is therefore not enough. Gertrude Stein was driven finally to an abstract art that would destroy her subject: the self-defeating absurdity of total abstraction. This is a crucial truth of her work.

In addition, however, to improper subject matter sterilized by abstraction, Miss Stein has another important resource. Here we can be scarcely more clear or concrete than she allows us to be, and she is neither clear nor concrete in her explication. It is perhaps best to call this the doctrine of "essence"—a term she herself uses on occasion in discussing it—the principle that the "essence" of people and objects and even events provides proper material for the descriptive realist. One must suppose, though she never says this in so many words, that "essence" is really synonymous with that "inner reality" she refers to in her creed.[32] "Essence," Miss Stein intimates, is that which makes a person or a thing what he or it is, the motivating, defining truth under the surface:

[32] Cf. text, p. 65.

I have of course always been struggling with this thing, to say what you nor I nor nobody knows, but what is really what you and I and everybody knows . . . in my portraits I had tried to tell what each one is without telling stories and now in my early plays I tried to tell what happened without telling stories so that the essence of what happened would be like the essence of the portraits, what made what happened be what it was.[33]

Again she says of her purpose in a particular play, "I wanted still more to tell what could be told if one did not tell anything."[34]

In order to relate these particular researches to her continuing concerns and to testify once more to the fact that she is still thinking coherently of the artist's duties to live "contemporaneously" and to strive for true creativity, we may cite one further passage:

I had to find out inside everyone what was in them that was intrinsically exciting and I had to find out not by what they said not by what they did not by how much or how little they resembled any other one but I had to find out by the intensity of movement that there was inside in any one of them. . . . I must find out what is moving inside them that makes them them, and I must find out how I by the thing moving excitedly inside in me can make a portrait of them.[35]

[33] Stein, "Plays," in *Lectures in America,* 121.
[34] *Ibid.,* 119.
[35] Stein, "Portraits and Repetition," in *Lectures in America,* 183.

In the characteristic "composition" of our time, essence proves to be "intensity of movement inside," a phrase difficult to pursue to a more tangible clarification. In perfect charity, however, it is vaguely possible to assume that Gertrude Stein may be seeking the same thing that a great artist must always seek: the ultimately unknowable truth that is historically and psychologically the "essence" of men and the combining of men into events. But I do not really think so. What she is after is an abstractly satisfactory "present knowing" of her subject, and that kind of knowing is in the first place perfectly subjective and in the second place almost perfectly incommunicable in Miss Stein's particular terms. At any rate, the textual difficulty here, as in so much of Miss Stein's theorizing, lies in her stubborn habit of defining her aims in the private language and logistics of idiosyncratic "genius."

Donald Sutherland applies what is probably his most impressive chapter, the third, to a spirited justification of these attitudes toward subject matter that I have been denouncing. The problem, as Mr. Sutherland treats it, is partly one of subject matter per se—what is proper matter for a writer after all—and partly one of the method of "expressing" that matter—in what manner is the writer to reduce his experience of his subject to the shape and language that makes it literature? The latter sense of the problem is more relevant to the subject matter of my next three chapters, and I will deal with it there at greater length. Mr. Sutherland centers his explication around the so-called "crazy book" of 1914, *Tender Buttons*. The volume is a set of still-life squibs in cubist language, divided into three compartments of "Objects Food Rooms," and it may be taken as fairly representative of that vein of radical abstraction which finally becomes Gertrude Stein's most characteristic métier.

Her great effort in *Tender Buttons,* as Donald Sutherland sees, was to apply the pragmatist concept of reality, "the direct sense of things as unique and unclassified,"[36] to the "Objects Food Rooms" that were her current units of experience. As we have seen, she wanted to immunize the "memory and identity" which she felt sentimentalized all conventional literary apprehension of a subject, and one way to accomplish this was to assault the name and the customary descriptive vocabulary of an object by rendering it into a private abstract language. Thus "much of the effort in *Tender Buttons* is to replace or shock the name of anything in order to restore the sense of immediate unprepared experience."[37]

Our immediate question is: What is the function of a given subject for Gertrude Stein and what becomes of it for the reader as she handles it? The answer is, in outline, very simple: a subject for Gertrude Stein is a stimulus, or a diving board, for a plunge into a new reality; the subject comes to the reader in the form of a difficult abstract art in which the original has been replaced by a "new reality" that is sometimes penetrable, sometimes not, sometimes interesting, sometimes perfectly dull. Gertrude

[36] Sutherland, *op. cit.,* 74.
[37] *Ibid.,* 75.

Stein would argue, and Donald Sutherland agrees, that the artist has no real responsibility to his subject; he can do with it anything he chooses. I think that is true, but I think it follows as well that everything he may do with it will not be of equal value. Thus while we cannot demand that a painter or a writer be as faithful to the camera sense of his object as, say, the Dutch genre painters, we can demand that the subjective sense which is his substitute be as interesting as the camera sense; we may very well ask that the "new reality" be as interesting as the old, the "sentimental" one.

It is perfectly true, as Mr. Sutherland says, that the artists' "initial vision of the subject matter is not the standard or practical vision of their contemporaries, and they are further governed by the impulse to make something of it, so that what may still be recognizable in the result is only an incident or a circumstance."[38] I also agree that "the appreciation and enjoyment of the result"[39] is that part of the artistic process which is the reader's province and responsibility. We must agree, that is, that any departure from an original subject or any degree of abstraction in vision or technique is justifiable, but only if we feel it as a functional process, one that adds to our knowledge or our understanding or our simple enjoyment of experience. I can only send the reader to Gertrude Stein's own abstract work for a decision. For me, generally, the subjective new reality I find there is no better than

[38] *Ibid.*, 79.
[39] *Ibid.*

the camera sense and is infinitely inferior to the sense I receive from Joyce or Proust or Virginia Woolf, who work at a level of abstraction that seems to me beautifully functional because it is electric and illuminating.

There is the further intricate question of whether Gertrude Stein is justified in applying to people, as she does, the same technique of extreme subjective abstraction that she applies to "Objects Food Rooms." I doubt it. In the conduct of life, the still-life elements are never of more than passing concern—or should not be. One cares little, after all, how one is directed to apprehend a Cutlet, a Cloak, a Cold Climate, or a Carafe; only a great master such as Cézanne or Picasso can rouse us to more than a sybaritic pleasure in objects on a table. But human beings are something else. We care passionately how human beings are disposed about the universe and how they are seen and how described. The technique that in *Tender Buttons* is intermittently interesting and generally tiresome, when applied to humanity in *The Making of Americans,* in the portraits and plays, in a "novel" like *Ida,* becomes thoroughly misleading and repugnant; the matter grows serious. Great writing teaches us about ourselves by displaying the race as mythic or heroic or satanic or simply commonplace and "true," but Gertrude Stein's technique takes life from her people. If they move at all, they walk like somnambulists; we cannot know them or know ourselves from them.

The great sin of Gertrude Stein's theory and the sin of Donald Sutherland's apology, as I see it, is that they tend to reduce life to a momentary and subjective sensation, to an elaborated dilettantism. They deny literature as a function of life aimed at complementing life by interpreting it to our intelligence and our emotions, to our conviction that we can know it and perhaps make it richer. When Mr. Sutherland says, "We know that literature is a different reality from life, and that it is differently organized,"[40] we can only agree with him. But we do not have to agree that "the world may be reasonably taken as a fair,"[41] which is to say that its meaning is sensation and that value judgments are unnecessary, or agree to respect art that "exists in and for itself,"[42] which is simply to reassert the respectability of art-for-art.

I, for one, cannot agree with Donald Sutherland's value structure when he says:

That an intonation does not last as long as the outline of the Sierra Nevada is not relevant to the immediate and final present. All the little things that in a longer perspective of time look trivial and transient and so negligible suddenly become as real as the president of the republic or original sin or the Rock of Gibraltar, and it is quite as delightful and urgent to the mind to define these little things, any group of them given together, as to articulate a political or a theological or an imperial system.[43]

[40] *Ibid.*, 80.
[41] *Ibid.*, 90.
[42] *Ibid.*, 91.
[43] *Ibid.*, 88.

More "delightful," I am sure, but to any but a dilettante mind, surely less "urgent." Mr. Sutherland is being silly. For aren't we more serious than this about literature? Don't we want it to supply us with a longer and larger truth than the momentary, private, and idiosyncratic? Not that we can ask literature to be life or to be uniformly serious and solemn and self-consciously moralistic; that is not the point. But I think we must, if we are serious about living, ask literature to be that part of life which observes life conceptually in search of usable truth, that it somehow interpret experience, that it supply us with data for generalization about our nature and our motives, and finally that it do these services in terms we can understand and, if we choose, apply.

We must also remember that Gertrude Stein carries the art-for-art position to its extreme, farther even than Donald Sutherland bothers to follow her. There is at last no real defense for this kind of aesthetics. Real art, she would have it, is not only a "different reality" from living, as we would all agree, but "an end in itself and in that respect it is opposed to the business of living." This, I think, very few would care to accept; there really is no time for an art that is opposed to the business of living. The rest of the problem is a matter of technique and expression, and we may reflect on these aspects of it in the course of our next three chapters.

5

PROPER AND IMPROPER TECHNIQUE:

What Is in Your Head Comes Down into Your Hand

Practically, when the doctrine of "essence" as proper subject matter moves from theory into writing, further problems at once appear. Clearly, the ectoplasmic compound Gertrude Stein calls essence is apprehensible only by a mystic or by a genius in art of the very first rank. She assures us that she is not a mystic but is most distinctly a genius.[1] Granting her genius for the moment, if we ask, first, whether such essence is at all communicable and, second, whether it is communicable in a private language, fundamental flaws at the very foundations of her art immediately confront us.

Turning now to the question of proper and improper technique, as distinguished from subject matter, we find that Miss Stein's insistence on the absoluteness of creativity again brings heavy consequences. We find, in

[1] Cf. text, pp. 168–70.

fact, just what we should have expected to find: a theory of the necessary spontaneity of the true creative utterance. The classical picture of the artist as the man who applies to his intellectual or imaginative vision a process of studied sharpenings and refinings—the artist as laborer—Miss Stein ruthlessly paints out. For her, as she puts it, "to try is to die."[2]

When Kenneth Burke says of *Lectures in America* that it is "complicated by the co-presence of its revision,"[3] he is being entirely accurate within our normal terminology. What he means is that the text includes throughout both the tentative statement of an idea and "corrected" versions of the idea, as many as needed. But Miss Stein would not admit the term "revision." The real artist does not revise; only "secondary" talents need do that. The true artist, in the state of perfect union of subject, self, and time, always records his ongoing present knowing. As Thornton Wilder has quoted her: "Artists do not experiment. . . . An artist puts down what he knows and at every moment it is what he knows at that moment. If he is trying things out to see how they go he is a bad artist."[4]

The secondary talent reflects upon his insight and re-orders it in revision; he is therefore doubly damned: if the knowledge had been true, it would have required no reflection or re-ordering, and in the gratuitous revision process he is guilty of process, a pastness that destroys any

[2] Stein, *Everybody's Autobiography,* 65.

[3] Kenneth Burke, "The Impartial Essence," *New Republic,* Vol. LXXXIII (July 3, 1935), 227.

[4] Wilder, Introduction to *Four in America,* by Gertrude Stein, vii.

shreds of truth that might have inhered in the original vision. The true artist, on the other hand, "knows what he knows when he knows it" and records his ongoing present

knowing. Thus the things Mr. Burke calls revision are for Gertrude Stein new knowing. Burke would suggest, of course, that she eliminate the earlier, faulty portions of her texts as they are made invalid or less valid by new insights. Miss Stein would say no, both old and new are true.

It is this doctrine that forces upon a reader conditioned to a careful art the sense of such intolerable areas of waste motion in Gertrude Stein's books. For example, a careful artist could take *The Making of Americans*, which runs to 416 closely printed pages in the "short" Harcourt, Brace edition of 1934, and compress all its basic narrative, its philosophical reflection, and its insight into character—in a word, its real matter—into no more than fifty pages, and one suspects that the condensed version would prove to be a little masterpiece of group biography. Miss Stein should have been instructed by the fact that the first version of this work, almost 600,000 words, was cut in half without organic damage, but she was not.

None of this implies that Gertrude Stein is, in the conventional sense, a slovenly writer. Few writers have ever worked harder, longer, more scientifically, or with a greater sense of holy mission at the effort of perfecting their recording mechanisms. Many passages in her writing testify to this unremitting struggle. "It was a long tormenting process," she says, "she looked, listened and described."[5] In writing the long first version of *The Making of Americans* she habitually worked in complete isolation from eleven at night until dawn, "struggling with her sentences, those long sentences that had to be so exactly carried out."[6] Her first book, *Three Lives,* was in the process of composition while Picasso was painting his famous portrait of her. This picture required "eighty or ninety" sittings, and Miss Stein tells us that "during these long poses and these long walks Gertrude Stein meditated and made sentences."[7] "Struggle" is a word that appears again and again in her descriptions of her writing process. The impression of slovenliness that one takes away from her work results, then, not from her laziness, but from an entirely conscious aesthetic position. She has fallen once more into a trap of her own making; one struggles toward the state of true creativity, but once confidently within it, one, by definition, admits to the page everything present in the consciousness, for that is the present knowing, the "creative recognition." One does not alter or select; one records, for all things are equally true and equally valuable. Hence the "co-presence of the revision" in *Lectures in America* and the copresence in all her books of things that are to the reader intolerably dull or thoroughly interesting, but among which Miss Stein refuses to select or excise.

Her real concern here is with her old enemy, time. Revision cannot be admitted to the creative process be-

[5] Stein, *The Autobiography of Alice B. Toklas,* 99.

[6] *Ibid.,* 35.

[7] *Ibid.,* 41.

cause it is another of those factors that force awareness of audience and identity, thereby diluting the perfect present knowing. Revision prevents the writer from "making what I know come out as I know it, come out not as remembering";[8] it prevents "the sense of immediacy."

The record of Gertrude Stein's opinion of revision is certainly very clear, and we should document two further instances that will take us into one of the regions of hot critical dispute about Miss Stein's work. The first passage comes from *Everybody's Autobiography:*

> *I like writing, it is so pleasant, to have the ink write it down on the paper as it goes on doing. Harlan Miller thought I left such a large space in between so that I could correct in between but I do not correct . . . after all what is in your head comes down into your hand and if it has come down it can never come again no not again.*[9]

Now a second passage from a conversation with John Hyde Preston, which we may quote extensively because it further develops these ideas and because it serves to remind us once more of Gertrude Stein's very real intelligence. Confronted with the stupefying quality of much of her work, one is likely to forget that behind it all lies a mind that is in many ways absolutely first rate. She is speaking to Preston, who has sought her out because he is discouraged with his own writing:

[8] Stein, "Portraits and Repetition," in *Lectures in America,* 181.
[9] Stein, *Everybody's Autobiography,* 311.

> *You will write . . . if you will write without thinking of the result in terms of a result, but think of the writing in terms of discovery, which is to say that creation must take place between the pen and the paper, not before in a thought or afterwards in a recasting. Yes, before in a thought, but not in careful thinking. It will come if it is there and if you will let it come, and if you have anything you will get a sudden creative recognition. You won't know how it was, even what it is, but it will be creation if it came out of the pen and out of you and not out of an architectural drawing of the thing you are doing. Technique is not so much a thing of form and style as the way that form and style came and how it can come again. Freeze your fountain and you will always have your frozen water shooting into the air and falling and it will be there to see—oh, no doubt of that—but there will be no more coming. . . . You cannot go into the womb to form the child; it is there and makes itself and comes forth whole—and there it is and you have made it and have felt it, but it has come itself—and that is creative recognition. Of course you have a little more control of your writing than that; you have to know what you want to get; but when you know that, let it take you and if it seems to take you off the track don't hold back, because that is perhaps where instinctively you want to be and if you hold back and try to be always where you have been before, you will go dry.*[10]

[10] Preston, "A Conversation," *Atlantic Monthly,* Vol. CLVI (August, 1935), 188.

Such phrasings as "what is in your head comes down into your hand," "creation must take place between the pen and the paper," and "it has come itself"—she has said similar things in other places—make one feel again that the relation between Gertrude Stein's subject and herself is uncomfortably close to the occult. We are also very close here to the critical dispute mentioned above. B. F. Skinner has developed the interesting thesis that some of Miss Stein's writing, specifically *Tender Buttons,* is not creation at all in the usual sense, but the product of "automatic writing."[11] He reaches this conclusion after comparing Miss Stein's later published writings with the results of her researches in automatic writing with Leon Solomons, under William James and Münsterberg at Radcliffe in 1896. Mr. Skinner makes such a thorough and persuasive defense of his position that one cannot safely dismiss it.

Gertrude Stein noticed Skinner's essay only to deride it mildly. "It was very amusing," she told the boys at the Choate School.[12] And in *Everybody's Autobiography* she says, "I did not think that we either of us had been doing automatic writing, we always knew what we were doing. . . . I did not think it was automatic I do not think so now."[13] She tells us also that the article in the *Psychological Review* detailing the researches,[14] though signed by

[11] B. F. Skinner, "Has Gertrude Stein A Secret?" *Atlantic Monthly,* Vol. CLIII (January, 1934), 50–57.
[12] Stein, "How Writing Is Written," in *The Oxford Anthology of American Literature,* II, 1449.
[13] Stein, *Everybody's Autobiography,* 266–67.
[14] Gertrude Stein and Leon M. Solomons, "Normal Motor Automatism," *Psychological Review,* Vol. III (September, 1896), 492–513.

both Solomons and Gertrude Stein, was actually written by Solomons alone.[15] Mr. Skinner was probably ignorant of this fact; on the basis of this ignorance and the unquestionable resemblance between *Tender Buttons* and some of the reported "automatic" writing—which Miss Stein contends was always conscious—he has drawn a logical but deceptive correlation.

We can refuse to accept Skinner's thesis simply because of Gertrude Stein's demurrer, but with her that is never a safe course. It has been demonstrated too often that her memory is a malleable instrument. If one discounts Skinner's theory, one should do so on textual evidence rather than on Miss Stein's own denial. It seems more logical to believe that both *Tender Buttons* and the "automatic" writing resulted from conscious effort—that their oddity results from the special eccentricity of that consciousness. Internal textual evidence indicates that while large portions of her work are bizarre enough to suggest some peculiar method of creation—automatism is as logical to suspect as any other—they are too clearly the result of an inclusive discipline to be the product of an unconscious state. Much of her work, unfortunately, is too dull to have sprung from the unconscious. Although the relation of Miss Stein to her subject does suggest the occult, one still feels that she always retains "a little more control of . . . writing than that" she recommends to Preston. And we still find her insisting, "No, writing should be very exact."[16]

[15] Stein, *Everybody's Autobiography*, 267.
[16] *Ibid.*

At this point we can pick up another dictum from the conversation with Preston to return us to the examination of Gertrude Stein's view of form as an aspect of technique: ". . . it will be creation if it came out of the pen and out of you and not out of an architectural drawing of the thing you are doing." Clearly we can no more expect architecture than we can expect revision in a work by Gertrude Stein. This is not to say that form is undesirable, but that it is of secondary importance, welcomed if it comes and unmourned if it is absent. Finally, form is to be coterminous with the artist's vision—his moment-to-moment knowing; it is unique, both with the artist and with the work at hand. Again, Miss Stein makes clear her conviction that the artist is the final arbiter and repository of value. "It is not the form but the fact that *you are the form* that is important," she tells Preston.[17]

All this adds up to the view that form is simply the fortuitous shape assumed by the unconstricted emergence of the poured-out bits of knowing. Hence the reader conditioned to expect architecture in writing, a sense of skeleton and outline and cohesion and destination, inevitably feels that Gertrude Stein's works are formless. A member of her Paris circle said of her first Cézanne—it was really Leo's—"you could tell it was finished because it had a frame";[18] the same judgment precisely describes many of her books: one can tell they are finished because they are

[17] Preston, "A Conversation," *Atlantic Monthly*, Vol. CLVI (August, 1935), 194; italics his.
[18] Stein, *The Autobiography of Alice B. Toklas*, 28.

in covers. We may note, parenthetically, that Miss Stein did not like to hang her pictures in frames, an attitude highly symptomatic of her characteristic rebellion against anything that can be interpreted as constriction imposed upon art or artist from without.

She conceives form as an enemy in the familiar pattern. It is contrary to the time sense of our generation, to its "composition"; consciousness of form forces consciousness of identity and audience and awareness of self, thus leading to faulty creativity. These sins are interrelated, as they always are for her, and they conflow, in turn, with the problem of subject matter I talked about under Miss Stein's heading of "events." Events provide poor subject matter, and combining events or happenings into a narrative story line is poor technique. Her reasoning emerges in a statement from one of her lectures at the University of Chicago:

> . . . *most writing has been a real narrative writing a telling of the story of anything in the way that thing has been happening and now everything is not that thing there is at present not a sense of anything being successively happening, moving is in every direction beginning and ending is not really exciting, anything is anything, anything is happening and anybody can know anything at any time that anything is happening and so really and truly is there any sentence and any paragraphing is there prose and poetry as the same thing is there now any narrative of any successive thing.* [19]

[19] Gertrude Stein, *Narration,* 19.

For an atomistic era, then, we must have an atomistic art: "moving is in every direction."

Gertrude Stein would accept Aristotle's definition of a whole as that which "has a beginning and middle and end," but she will have none of the notion that a whole is a desirable thing. Wholes themselves are culpable on the expected grounds: " . . . a whole thing is not interesting because as a whole well as a whole there has to be remembering and forgetting."[20] Miss Stein worried long and seriously about beginning and middle and ending, for these are the elements that make a whole, and a whole is wrong because it presupposes a planned form, and a planned form presupposes the things that create audience and identity and imperfect art:

> *Now you take anything that is written and you read it as a whole it is not interesting it begins as if it is interesting but it is not interesting because if it is going to have a beginning and middle and ending it has to do with remembering and forgetting and remembering and forgeting is not interesting it is occupying but it is not interesting.*[21]

It is amusing to see that she now becomes involved in exactly the same paradox that confronted her in evaluating subject matter. Just as her improper subject matter became her inevitable subject matter, so her improper

20 Stein, *The Geographical History of America,* 115.
21 *Ibid.*, 114.

form becomes her inevitable form. Because without beginning and ending nothing comes into being or ever ceases, one submits to them:

And yet after all . . . master-pieces have to use beginning and ending to become existing . . . anybody who is trying to do anything today is desperately not having a beginning and ending but nevertheless in some way one does have to stop. I stop.[22]

She begins, too, but petulantly and grudgingly, for the despairing reason that if she does not, her work does not exist.

Not unexpectedly, Miss Stein deals with the paradox of form just as she dealt with the paradox of subject matter. Just as she disguised her objective subject by a moderate degree of abstraction or contemptuously obliterated it by an extreme degree of abstraction, so she disguises or obliterates her beginnings and endings and even middles until they are destroyed as conscious form, destroyed in every sense except that in which they are beyond her control, the odious physical necessity of imprinting the first and last letter of the work at hand.

She masks her beginnings by plunging *in medias res* or by starting at a point not visibly connected with her essential matter or, even more characteristically, by using endless rebeginnings that flow back to or beyond her point of first departure, surrounding and submerging it, completely destroying the sense of chronology, and erasing

[22] Stein, "What Are Masterpieces," in *What Are Masterpieces*, 89.

the original beginning as a finite point in the consciousness of the reader.

She masks her endings in the same basic ways. She may, for example, pull a work to an abrupt and arbitrary halt. "Now that is all," she says at the end of "Composition as Explanation"; "And so this is just at present all I know about the theatre," she writes at the end of "Plays"; "Now I am not sure that is not all," are the last words of *The Geographical History of America.* Or she stops when she comes to a point that is meaningful to her rather than to her audience: "I might have told you more in detail but in that case you would that is I would not have as clearly seen as I do now what an oil painting is."[23] What is more important, she uses many devices to prevent the reader's having the sense of orderly progress toward an end; she abjures suspenseful narrative sequences or logical cause-effect patterns: "Question and answer make you know time is existing."[24] She includes a number of real or apparent irrelevancies and *non sequitur's* and makes many redoublings on the chronological path—always denying the reader's ancient prerogative of expecting a destination.

When we look at the "middles" of Gertrude Stein's works—and we may as well use the term as loosely as she herself does, including in it everything not specifically a beginning or end, the real body of all her work—we are soon painfully conscious of what seems the most char-

[23] Gertrude Stein, "Pictures," in *Lectures in America,* 90.
[24] Stein, *Everybody's Autobiography,* 244.

acteristic trait of her style: its flatness. Generally speaking, Miss Stein's prose is almost completely lacking in modulation: in color, in nuance, in problem and resolution, climax and denouement, tension and release, in rise and fall, light and shade. That all this is conscious with her, that it has a philosophical basis, and that she conceives it as proper technique becomes clear when we examine her aesthetic statements. The pervasive flatness develops partly as a consequence of her point of observation, partly as a result of her notion of what constitutes proper prose movement, and partly as a culmination of her theories of language. By tracing her approach to these problems, we may conclude this account of Gertrude Stein's ideas on proper technique, but we must travel a long and thorny way.

An extremely interesting case could be made for the idea that the characteristic point of observation of the artist has undergone a species of revolution in the twentieth century. Classically, the artist observes from a position bound to earth, eye-to-eye and hand-to-hand with his fellows, in contact by touch or sight with irregularities in the earth or with structures raised upon it, and his art is directed by a sense awareness of his environment, by the proportions and perspectives reported by the eye from six feet above the surface of the earth. The heavens are his unknown. It is far from inconceivable that the twentieth-century liberation of man from the earth and his transubstantiation in his former unknown have effected a revolution in sensibility of which he is in some degree conscious.

Reality is seen with the eye of the bird—the man in the airplane—with all the attendant consequences of distortions, flattening, geometrizing, and disconnectedness that largely compose the abstraction of art in our time.

We need not suggest categorically that Gertrude Stein conceived the bird's-eye view as the necessary point of observation for the twentieth-century artist. She seems never to have pursued it quite that far. But there can be no doubt that her later thinking moved in this direction. The truth of the matter seems to be that this idea came to her, half-formed, with the force of revelation during her airplane tour of the United States in 1934–35 as she watched American topography roll out beneath her, abstracted and geometrized and dramatized, and that she did a great deal of thinking back under the stimulus of this experience, and concluded, largely through hindsight, that such a theory had all along been basic to her principles of abstraction. Although most of her thinking is *post hoc* here, she interpreted it as confirming some of her earlier ideas about abstraction, particularly abstraction as an American phenomenon.

Gertrude Stein had long subscribed to the theory —which is at least as old as Demetrius and as modern as Taine—of the intimate interrelationship of geography and art. As she herself puts it: "After all anybody is as their land and air is. Anybody is as the sky is low or high, the air heavy or clear and anybody is as there is wind or no wind there. It is that which makes them and the arts they make."[25] Seeing America from an airplane confirmed her conviction that the geography of America was one that made abstraction the natural technique for the creative spirit. But apparently she had always seen it from the plane's-eye view as a land that wandered, free of constricting form, not bounded at all in any sensible way; vast, flat, with few landmarks, and so predominantly featureless that many boundaries were arbitrary straight lines drawn with a ruler on a map.

She felt as well that America lacked the feeling of insularity, the feeling of a hovering ceiling of sky that closed in Britain and the countries of Europe, forcing them to a hermetic "daily living" that became the essence of their lives and their art. In America, by contrast, "there is no sky, there is air,"[26] and this inherited lidlessness plus the absence of all but arbitrary boundaries, meant that the American was liberated in body and in mind: free in body to move in any direction—back and forth, in and out, up and down—the "moving . . . in every direction" characteristic of our century, which, remember, is the American century; free in mind to create an art that was not in servitude to the form and subject matter of "daily living" but able to move in the abstracted, private present knowing of true art. American geography frees the American artist for the realization of the necessary "lack of connection," the "disembodied way of disconnecting something from anything."[27] One feels, I think, that here Ger-

25 Stein, "An American and France," in *What Are Masterpieces,* 62.
26 Stein, *Everybody's Autobiography,* 202.
27 Stein, "What Is English Literature," in *Lectures in America,* 53.

trude Stein has a sound and impressive intuition about our country and our time. But how to transmute it into a verbal art? How to express it?

In the "disembodied" bird's-eye or plane's-eye view of reality, at any rate, reality is flat, and it is this flatness that concerns us here. Gertrude Stein made the point of observation that sees things as flat an important part of her theory of proper technique. The artist must see reality as flat because, in the first place, he is "contemporaneous" to flatness and, secondly, because he must record it as part of the "composition" of his time. Now, by an important extension, the artist takes this necessity and makes it a formal virtue. He takes the sense of flatness and applies it as technique to his subject matter; he suppresses its undulations into featureless flatness, thereby suppressing all its inequalities and all its chiaroscuro, until he is able to eliminate modulation as an objective thing, a thing in itself capable of making him know he is knowing it. It is the familiar argument, made an aspect of technique: "The human mind has neither identity nor time and when it sees anything has to look flat."[28] The artist flattens the features of his subject because their prominence can make him conscious that he is using a subject to create art.

The doctrine returns us, naturally enough, to Miss Stein's bugbears of the inevitable prose landmarks of a beginning, a middle, and an end. Flattening the features of the subject, particularly the rise and fall of events, can help to prevent awareness of these skeletal members of the work:

> *. . . the human mind . . . always . . . is trying to make it be to itself that human nature is interesting but it is not and so the master-pieces always flatten it out, flatten human nature out so that there is no beginning and middle and ending, because if there is not then there is no doing and if there is no doing then there is no human nature.*[29]

This highly abstruse element of Gertrude Stein's aesthetics is worth detailing at length because it is basic to the fundamental air of her style, its flatness. She aimed, consciously and philosophically, at an art without outline or skeleton or topography. Inevitably, to the reader, that art is amoeboid.

28 Stein, *The Geographical History of America,* 147.
29 *Ibid.,* 158.

6
THEORIES OF MOVEMENT:
Moving Is in Every Direction

We must look next at the contribution Gertrude Stein's theories of movement make to the general featurelessness of her style. When we begin to trace her statements on prose movement, we find that new distinctions are necessary. Miss Stein found that three basic kinds of movement were palatable to her: movement as succession, movement "within" or self-contained, and a directionless movement that finally reduced itself to stasis. She isolated these three types as she moved slowly through her early years as a writer, and a rough chronological division of her early works can be made on the basis of the types; in her later works it becomes increasingly difficult to separate the three forms. The important thing to note at the outset is that her effort to define the three movements harmonizes easily with her continuing preoccupation with the parent problems of "contemporaneousness" and the "whole present," and they, of course, overlap with the related properties of subject matter already discussed.

If we set aside Gertrude Stein's first and best book, *Three Lives*, in which she seems to have been only semi-conscious of matters that were later to be her great aesthetic concerns—in it, as she tells us, there was only "a groping for a continuous present"[1]—we find that her serious struggles with the problems of time and movement begin immediately. The three years of concentrated labor devoted to *The Making of Americans* brought all these principles to a focus. Here she began the struggle, which continued for forty years, to achieve "the sense of immediacy" and "to make what I know come out as I know it, come out not as remembering." This was first a problem of subject matter, as we have already suggested, that Miss Stein believed she had solved by a progressively greater suppression, amounting at last to obliteration, of the story element in her work. But it was also a problem of technique that involved the sense of movement. Her solution of it in this sense is very interesting as theory, though often paralyzing as art.

Gertrude Stein makes an illuminating comparison of her first solution of the movement dilemma with the contemporary solution offered by the cinema. She was not "influenced" by cinematic technique, she tells us—"I doubt whether at that time I had seen a cinema"[2]—but she and the cinema proceeded in similar ways. For Miss

[1] Stein, "Composition as Explanation," in *What Are Masterpieces*, 32.
[2] Stein, "Portraits and Repetition," in *Lectures in America*, 177.

Stein this is one more proof of the inevitable "contemporaneousness" of a man and his era: "Any one is of one's period and this our period was undoubtedly the period of the cinema."[3] At any rate, Miss Stein reached a temporary reconciliation with movement:

. . . by listening and talking I conceived at every moment the existence of some one, and I put down each moment that I had the existence of that one inside in me.[4]

She relates the problem to cinema technique thus:

I was doing what the cinema was doing, I was making a continuous succession of the statement of what that person was until I had not many things but one thing.[5]

The analogy collapses if we try to carry it beyond the simple matter of successive "statements." Gertrude Stein by no means makes successive objective "images" in the cinema sense. Her statements "of what that person was" are mere semantic abstractions, although she would not admit the fact, of her private "knowing." Nor can we carry the analogy to the cinema technique of stringing images along a story line. She suppresses, as much as she possibly can, any rise and fall or beginning, middle, and end. Endings, for example, are made to coincide arbi-

[3] *Ibid.*
[4] *Ibid.*, 198.
[5] *Ibid.*, 176–77.

trarily with the collapse of the artist's attention to his subject, which has, incidentally, long ago become objectively invisible: "So finally I was emptied of saying this thing, and so no longer said what they were."[6]

Inevitably all these idiosyncrasies contribute to the pervasive flatness of Miss Stein's style. It is also easy to see how the cinematic technique of a rapid succession of infinitesimally differentiated states of knowing would appear on the printed page as repetition. It does just that, and it becomes a very heavy factor in her flatness of style. In theorizing about repetition, Miss Stein plumbs the most sophistical depths of her aesthetics. We can begin our analysis of the problem here with a fair sample of her true repetitive manner taken from *The Making of Americans*. A fair sample, however, is not strictly possible; the full paralyzing effect of such writing can be felt only if one takes it in the overpowering mass in which Miss Stein serves it. There are 416 pages of this in the shortened version; in the first version, there are 925 pages:

As I was saying Martha Hersland was all through her younger living of the feeling and the living of, for her natural family living, poor people. She was of the daily feeling and the daily living of them more than she was of the daily feeling and the daily living of her family living and feeling. She was then as I was saying of the daily living and the daily feeling of the people near her who had in them as I said of them half city feeling and half coun-

[6] *Ibid.*, 185.

try feeling. She was as I was saying as much as there was in her then of feeling and living of their feeling and their living. She was with them often in the evening, she was with them more or less in the daytime, she was of their daily living and their daily feeling more than she was then of any other feeling or living. As I was just saying she was with them often in the evening when she was not any longer a very young one, she was with them very much of the day-time, she was as I was saying of their daily living and their daily feeling almost all the daily living and the daily feeling there was in her then.

She was with them as I was just saying often in the evening now that she was no longer a very little one and very much of the day-time.[7]

It seems safe to say that this passage contains some of the flattest prose ever written and that it is repetitive. Gertrude Stein would accept the first part of this charge and, for reasons we have reviewed, lay it up to her credit rather than her debit; that it is repetitive, however, she would deny absolutely. Forced finally to take cognizance of the charge of repetition from readers everywhere, she demonstrated her usual adroitness in defense. Literally, of course, this is not repetition in the broken-record sense, and on this shred of truth she builds an elaborate rationale. The minute degrees of shift and change that one sees in the passage above are consonant with the artist's moment-

[7] Stein, *The Making of Americans*, 249.

to-moment advance in insight, and they therefore emerge for her as the literal record of her knowing.

Miss Stein carried her defense even further; she
111 went so far as to insist that there is literally no such thing as repetition in her kind of art. There is repetition in impure art, which only flatters itself that it does not repeat. The truly repetitive elements in literature are story elements: "They do not think their succeeding or failing is what makes repetition . . . that what happens makes repetition."[8] She continues to think along a familiar line: "anything one is remembering is a repetition."[9] Her alternative is to regard her kind of verbalizing not as repetition, but as "insistence"; and "insistence," though it repeats words, repeats no true matter, for it is the record of the ongoing present knowing of the true artist; it therefore remains ever new and ever true, though it may manifest itself in repeated words as the perfect subject-artist-time ball rolls along:

> *If this existence is this thing is actually existing there can be no repetition.*[10]

> *And so it is never necessary to say anything again as remembering but it is always said again because every time it is so it is so.*[11]

[8] Stein, "Portraits and Repetition," in *Lectures in America,* 194.
[9] *Ibid.,* 179.
[10] *Ibid.,* 170.
[11] Stein, *The Geographical History of America,* 85.

I have said that her thinking here is sophistical, but again this is not strictly true. The rationale of her repetitive or "insistent" style is symptomatic of a deadlier disease than sophistry. It is another manifestation of her schizophrenic divorce of aesthetics and art and offers an extreme instance of the thing that finally damns her as an artist. It is her colossal blind spot, her refusal, or perhaps her real inability, to recognize the inescapable gap between the sensorium of a private, idiosyncratic thinker and writer and the sensorium of an audience that has to make its peace not with the process or the theory, but with the end product. Inevitably, her "insistence" is our repetition, and the result is not art but anodyne.

Her first efforts, then, at solving the technical problem of movement were an "elaboration of the complexities of using everything and of a continuous present and of beginning again and again and again."[12] This method worked out in practice as the statement, in cinematic succession, of the ongoing moment of knowledge in "an enormously long thing," *The Making of Americans,* and "an enormously short thing,"[13] the early portraits. Her early idealistic purpose had been that of arriving at an "explanation" of the race by a "description" of it,[14] but idealism, at least in its humanitarian character, Miss Stein very quickly sloughed off. Having convinced herself that a "de-

[12] Stein, "Composition as Explanation," in *What Are Masterpieces,* 32.
[13] *Ibid.,* 32–33.
[14] Stein, "The Gradual Making of The Making of Americans," in *Selected Writings,* 215.

scription" of the race was a feasible thing, she "lost interest in it . . . it being my nature, I wanted to tear it down."[15]

Gertrude Stein could not fail to be uncomfortable with her cinematic technique. While she had been able to rationalize a fairly long acceptance of it, that method was still perilously close to a story line and a time awareness. She felt that she had to move toward a new technique for realization of movement. Although the reader has great difficulty in separating one manner from another, Miss Stein finds the differences very distinct:

And after that what changes what changes after that, after that what changes and what changes after that and after that and what changes and after that and what changes after that.[16]

The new variation, which we have called movement "within" or self-contained, relates itself as subject matter to Miss Stein's doctrine of "essence." Essence and movement within finally emerge as identical, as we saw earlier: "what is moving inside them that makes them them." It was this essence-movement that Miss Stein advocated as one of the basic subject matters for the artist in our era bent on realizing his "contemporaneousness": "We in this period have . . . living in moving being necessarily so intense that existing is indeed something, is in-

[15] Stein, "How Writing Is Written," in *The Oxford Anthology of American Literature,* II, 1451.

[16] Stein, "Composition as Explanation," in *What Are Masterpieces,* 33.

deed that thing that we are doing."[17] The peculiarity of movement in the twentieth century, it will be remembered, is its unique intensity, an intensity so great that it has meaning and is realizable without a setting in the time and space context that has historically been necessary for the apprehension of movement. This becomes a problem of technique when it comes to the point of actual formulation in a work of art, and Gertrude Stein welcomed this peculiarity of movement because she was free to realize essence without the things that cause awareness of identity and audience: free to ignore setting in space in setting of physical scene, free to ignore setting in time in the maintenance of a chronological story line. She worked at this technique in *A Long Gay Book*, in a new kind of portrait, and finally in *Tender Buttons*. The several techniques of movement cannot be followed chronologically in Miss Stein's work beyond this point, roughly 1913, for she alternates and even mingles her several manners; she is constantly "beginning again and again and again." The difficulty of identifying movement "within" can probably best be understood if we look at one of her clearer definitions of it:

> *. . . all that was necessary was that there was something completely contained within itself and being contained within itself was moving, not moving in relation to anything, not moving in relation to itself but just moving.*[18]

[17] Stein, "Portraits and Repetition," in *Lectures in America*, 182.
[18] *Ibid.*, 202.

Explication of the writing produced on the theory of movement "within" is impossible in any practical sense. It is understandable in terms of nothing else that one has ever read; it is absolutely *sui generis,* and one can only read the works themselves and labor for one's own enlightenment. However, we can discuss the matter as theory, our real purpose here.

The heart of the doctrine and its relation to the flatness of Miss Stein's style are contained in several of the abstract statements in *The Geographical History of America,* and the doctrine is nothing if not abstract:

> . . . *only the things flying around are interesting which makes the universe . . . flat land and the human mind, of course they do they do fly around.*[19]

> *The human mind does not hop around but it flies around.*[20]

> *If anything flies around there is no ending and no begun.*[21]

A number of the complicated, interrelated, and by now familiar principles of Gertrude Stein come together in these dense lines. The "flying around" connects itself, first, with the "moving is in every direction" that Miss Stein saw as the characteristic movement of our atomistic,

19 Stein, *The Geographical History of America,* 139.
20 *Ibid.,* 141.
21 *Ibid.*

space-time era, and, second, with her admiration for the plane's-eye point of observation from above. It carries us to the logical consequence of this point of observation: the flattening of the real world to the senses. For a time then, at least, the ideal movement for Gertrude Stein was one that by "flying around" removed any sense of direction or destination or recognizable space location, one that by "flying" rather than "hopping" suppressed all feeling of regular, planful, orderly moving along an undulating narrative line.

Unfortunately, the complication does not end there, for in converting the theory into technique, the artist unavoidably uses his private stock of intelligence and sense equipment. As Miss Stein puts it, "I must find out how I by the thing moving excitedly inside in me can make a portrait of them."[22] The rub comes, of course, in communicating this state, in reducing it to language. In practice Gertrude Stein recorded her knowledge of the essence movement of her subject in words that were for her consonant with that knowledge. This language is difficult to describe, for it is not expository, or descriptive, or connotative in the usual way; it is predominantly abstract and painterly. The best one can do is to look at a sample; the first of the "objects" in *Tender Buttons,* "A Carafe, That Is a Blind Glass," will serve as well as any:

A kind in glass and a cousin, a spectacle and nothing strange a single hurt color and an arrangement in a sys-

[22] Stein, "Portraits and Repetition," in *Lectures in America,* 183.

tem to painting. All this and not ordinary, not unordered in not resembling. The difference is spreading.[23]

This is one of the "things . . . in itself folded itself up inside itself . . . to be another thing which is that thing inside in that thing."[24] The kinship of this technique to cubism in painting is very clear and very interesting, and as literature it is by no means entirely opaque. It represents Miss Stein's point of closest approach to painting and almost the last point at which her abstract manner, remains either significantly communicable or stimulating. We must note, at any rate, the essential privateness of the vision and the flatness that results from the philosophical pursuit of featurelessness through the masking and distortion of objective landmarks in the subject.

Gertrude Stein's third theory of movement achieves importance mainly in her "plays." She wrote scores of things she called plays. A very few, such as *Yes Is for a Very Young Man,* roughly follow the form we normally regard as dramatic; a larger group, of which the best known is *Four Saints in Three Acts,* are really poetic tableaux; then there is a variegated host that vary in length from a few lines to several pages, plays in no intelligible sense, but mere fortuitous extensions of Miss Stein's mood of the moment. The middle group possess the greatest interest in her new theory of movement.

Miss Stein was motivated in her new tack by a

[23] Gertrude Stein, *Tender Buttons,* in *Selected Writings,* 407.
[24] Stein, "Portraits and Repetition," in *Lectures in America,* 200.

thoroughly original and important aesthetic concern. She found herself seriously troubled by the feeling, which most of us have subconsciously had, of the unfortunate gap between the time sense and emotion contained within the action of a play and the time sense and emotion of the audience, who are spectators of the action. She puts the matter very clearly:

> *. . . the scene as depicted on the stage is . . . almost always in syncopated time in relation to the emotion of everybody in the audience . . . your emotion concerning that play is always either behind or ahead of the play. . . . So your emotion is never going on at the same time as the action of the play.*[25]

In discussing Miss Stein's third theory of movement, we can begin with the dictum that represents her final position: "The better the play the more static."[26] By a logical extension this proposition led her to the suspicion that in our time prose and poetry are coming to be the same thing. That is, prose, which has traditionally been a *verb* state in that it is basically active—descriptive, analytical, or narrative—by undergoing her revolution, which strips it of movement in space, finally becomes indistinguishable from poetry, a *noun* state, a static thing having to do with naming. She also felt that she had revolutionized poetry by lifting it from its craven

[25] Stein, "Plays," in *Lectures in America*, 93.
[26] Stein, "How Writing Is Written," in *The Oxford Anthology of American Literature*, II, 1451.

naming function; poetry and prose thus refurbished are able to confront the realization of the self-canceling static movement that was her final ideal. Although it is perhaps impossible to make all this clear in normal exposition, we can, at any rate, struggle with it more fruitfully when we cope with Miss Stein's theories of language.

The theory of a kind of movement proper to plays is actually a good deal simpler and more readily intelligible than Miss Stein's doctrine of movement "within." She felt that the root of the difficulty, the "syncopated" relationship of audience emotion to stage emotion, lay in the "story" element of the play. The fact that a narrative-dramatic event-sequence was taking place on the stage meant that for a convincing counterfeiting of life, the actors had to "make acquaintance," as she puts it, with each other; the audience, on the other hand, had to "make acquaintance" with the action and the actors. This situation meant that there were, so to speak, three senses of time coexistent: that of the characters on the stage, the private time sense that each spectator inevitably brought to the theater with him, and the imperfect time sense of their "syncopated" comingling. The bête noire, Miss Stein believed, was the story, the successive events of the dramatic action. If this could be removed, then the characters would have no need of "making acquaintance" with each other; they would become part of the furniture of the scene, which could be incorporated without difficulty into the time sense of the spectator.

It will be remembered that Gertrude Stein had

already eliminated "events," both as subject matter and technique, as improper for an age in which events are so many that they are commonplace, dull, and meaningless because they have no part in the true "composition" of our era. It was then comparatively easy for her to eliminate them from her plays and to make a technical virtue of their absence. She wanted now, she tells us, "to tell what could be told if one did not tell anything."[27] She conceived the notion of the play-as-landscape; that is, a play without plot and without consecutive, purposeful movement. In this kind of play the relationship of the characters becomes comparable to that of the elements in a landscape —one of mere physical contiguity—static and presenting no time conflict:

The landscape has its formation and as after all a play has to have formation and be in relation one thing to the other thing and as the story is not the thing . . . then the landscape not moving but being . . . in relation, the trees to the hills the hills to the fields the trees to each other any piece of it to any sky. . . . And of that relation I wanted to make a play and I did, a great number of plays.[28]

The capital work in this manner is *Four Saints in Three Acts,* which, when set to music by Virgil Thompson and performed by a Negro cast in 1934, contributed greatly to Gertrude Stein's fame.

[27] Stein, "Plays," in *Lectures in America,* 119.
[28] *Ibid.,* 125.

The movement proper to this form was one "not moving but being always in relation," a movement not of continuity but of flux, a "moving . . . in every direction" that was ultimately—and this is the real definition of her third manner—a negation and cancellation of movement, reducing itself, practically, to the ideal stasis of the landscape and removing the problem of syncopated time: ". . . the movement in it was like a movement in and out with which anybody looking on can keep in time."[29] Finally, she says happily, "it is exciting and moves but it also stays."[30]

In any case, the complete and, to Gertrude Stein, desirable absence of feature and destination and the essential flatness of such a manner are obvious. Miss Stein's is still an art by subtraction.

[29] *Ibid.*, 131.
[30] *Ibid.*

7
THEORIES OF LANGUAGE:
I Wish Writing Would Not Sound Like Writing

We should look now at Gertrude Stein's theory of language and its character as proper technique and as the definitive component of the flatness of her style. Again, for explication, we are forced to subdivide the problem arbitrarily. I should therefore like to examine in turn her vocabulary, the sound element of her language, her ideas on punctuation, and her notion of the relationship of prose and poetry. Practically, of course, the problem of language is separable from no portion of Miss Stein's aesthetics or her art, but she herself made the great mistake of proceeding as if it were, and this is a cardinal fact for the critic. Language, the only thing by which we can apprehend her, was a thing to which she submitted grudgingly. Her brother Leo obviously oversteps when he suggests that she embarked upon obscurantist abstraction because she was unable to cope with language at even a rudimentary level.[1]

Her handling of the language is a consequence, not of incapacity, but of philosophical conviction—surely a mistaken conviction. At any rate, it is in the area of language that we can best see the full degree and the final absurdity of her cultivated superiority to the needs and limitations of a reader.

Miss Stein herself voices the pathos of her position: "I wish writing would not sound like writing and yet what else can any writing sound like."[2] She is trapped for the third time in the paradox of the improper becoming the inescapable. Why should writing not sound like writing? For the old reasons:

> . . . *if it sounds like writing then anybody can see it being written, and the human mind nobody sees the human mind while it is being existing, and master-pieces . . . may not be other than that they do not exist as anybody seeing them and yet there they are.*
>
> *Please please me.*
>
> *Anybody can please me, but that is not what the human mind is.*[3]

What she is saying here is that writing that "sounds like writing" results from the writer's awareness of an audience —one who says, "Please please me"—and from the writer's attempt to placate or satisfy the expectation of that

[1] Leo Stein, *op. cit.*, 136–37, 141–42.

[2] Stein, *The Geographical History of America*, 146.

[3] *Ibid.*

audience. An audience brings in its train its henchmen, memory and identity, and the three set about to belabor the integrity of the artist and to destroy the time-free perfection of his vision.

But because Gertrude Stein had decided she was a writer, she had to use language, and to that degree her writing had to "sound like writing." Very characteristically, then, she went seriously and scientifically and philosophically to work to make a virtue, once more, of necessity: she would make her writing sound as little like "writing" as she possibly could. This statement can be made in all seriousness; we can document her effort. As always, she moved largely by subtraction.

She proceeded to eliminate an audience for her writing by a complicated series of stratagems. One thing, clearly, that characterized the writing of "human nature" as distinct from that of the "human mind" was the attempt to placate a reader by giving him a sense of design, a sense of an orderly, planful whole. Miss Stein discovered the antidote to this conventional practice in an extremely interesting way:

I found that any kind of a book if you read with glasses and somebody is cutting your hair and so you cannot keep the glasses on and you use the glasses as a magnifying glass and so read word by word reading word by word makes the writing that is not anything be something.

Very regrettable but very true.

So that shows you that a whole thing is not in-

teresting because as a whole well as a whole there has to be remembering and forgetting, but one at a time, oh one at a time is something oh yes definitely something.[4]

Probably no other single passage in Gertrude Stein's entire work shows so clearly just how deeply the tendency to abstractness had penetrated her whole view of the world of reality and of art.

She concludes, then, that she will use her words "one at a time." That is, she will lay them on the line one after another, but not as parts of a larger unit; they will not be elements in a logical sequence. The meaning, the relevance, the function of each word is completely self-contained:

It carefully comes about that there is no identity and no time and therefore no human nature when words are apart.

Or rather when words are together.[5]

She will put them together physically, but essentially they will remain apart in significance. The "presentness" of this manner is clear, but unfortunately the flatness and the incommunicability are also clear. This technique is not active everywhere in Gertrude Stein's work, but it does act in large and characteristic portions of it. The disconnectedness of much of Miss Stein's prose is the result, then, not of accident or incapacity, but of a highly studied technique.

[4] *Ibid.*, 115.
[5] *Ibid.*, 168–69.

The poverty of Gertrude Stein's creative vocabulary oppresses everyone except the most charitable reader. The fact that she seems to work with no more than two or three hundred very ordinary words constitutes the most important single source of the drabness of her prose, more important than its point of observation or its peculiarities of movement. The poverty becomes all the more oppressive and mystifying when one reads those of her writings which are not consciously creative, or when one sees records of her performance in conversation. For Gertrude Stein was a highly literate woman; she commanded a vocabulary that was extensive, flexible, and capable of abundant clarity and force. One is driven to conclude that hers is a voluntary poverty, like that of the saints (a "secular saint," Donald Sutherland calls her), and that we are still being served an art by subtraction. The truth of this judgment can be documented.

In the act of creating, Gertrude Stein went through a disciplined process of stripping down her vocabulary until it became uniquely her own instrument, uniquely fitted to be the vehicle of her private conception of what was right for her art and pointedly designed not to satisfy but to defeat an audience equipped with a separate set of words and a separate set of expectations. My contention is supported by a very interesting group of her pronouncements.

We need to keep clearly in mind now, as always, Miss Stein's statement that she was fundamentally concerned with "exactitude." This clarifies the sequence of her ideas on language, and it also serves the important purpose of showing just how wrong are the many commentators who have contended that she aimed to "enrich" our language by adding to its associational and connotative resources. As perceptive a critic as Edmund Wilson, for example, fooled into thinking this was her design, included Miss Stein in *Axel's Castle* in his studies of writers who did have this purpose. On this score, however, Gertrude Stein makes her position very clear. What she wanted in contrast to Wilson's Symbolists, for example, was to limit language as narrowly as she could. In her lecture at the Choate School she spoke this way:

> *. . . the novels of the Nineteenth Century live by association; they are wont to call up other pictures than the one they present to you. I didn't want, when I said 'water,' to have you think of running water. Therefore I began limiting my vocabulary, because I wanted to get rid of anything except the picture within the frame. . . . I didn't want, when I used one word, to make it carry with it too many associations. I wanted as far as possible to make it exact, as exact as mathematics; that is to say, for example, if one and one make two, I wanted to get words to have as much exactness as that. . . . The whole history of my work has been a history of that. I made a great many discoveries, but the thing that I was always trying to do was this thing.*[6]

[6] Stein, "How Writing Is Written," in *The Oxford Anthology of American Literature*, II, 1450.

It is, of course, true that enrichment of language does not need to proceed by multiplication and that there is a kind of enrichment which moves toward accuracy by excising impedimenta; but, lest we assume too quickly that Gertrude Stein was aiming at a thing we have learned to respect, the spare, surgically precise style of a Flaubert or a Hemingway, we should pursue the matter further. Miss Stein was an enemy not alone of Euphues, but of Flaubert as well. The "exactness" that Miss Stein claims as her purpose here has to be redefined. It is not the Flaubertian *mot juste,* chiseled for perfect accuracy and nuance of communication between writer and reader. Instead, it returns once again to the idiosyncratic sensorium: this exactness is to be Gertrude Stein's exactness. If it emerges as exactness to the reader, it will do so by accident. The reader, at any rate the reader conditioned to "literature," is the enemy.

Miss Stein's statements of her theory and method are very interesting, and we should examine them at considerable length. First, an example from one of her lectures in America:

I began to wonder . . . just what one saw when one looked at anything really looked at anything. Did one see sound, and what was the relation of color and sound, did it make itself by description by a word that meant it or did it make itself by a word in itself. All this time I was of course not interested in emotion or that anything happened. . . .[7]

[7] Stein, "Portraits and Repetition," in *Lectures in America,* 191.

> *. . . the word or words that made what I looked at be itself were always words that to me very exactly related themselves to that thing the thing at which I was looking, but as often as not had as I say nothing whatever to do with what any words would do that described that thing.*[8]

The key words here, as always with Gertrude Stein, are "to me." This is the method of selecting language designed to give rise to what Julian Sawyer, one of Miss Stein's more hysterical admirers, calls the "automatic and spontaneous synonymy of word and thing."[9] Sawyer does not blink at the fact that most of us are equipped only with words that "mean it" and "describe that thing"; but, as he sees it, if we fail to follow Miss Stein, ours is the fault, not hers; we are trying to evaluate in the light of our "lack of perception" the "absolute perspicacity of the most important writer writing today."[10]

At any rate, Gertrude Stein, in search of "exactness," used "words that very exactly related themselves to that thing." These words, "as often as not," proved to be completely aloof from traditional descriptive terminology. Such a practice contributes heavily to both the poverty and the eccentricity of her creative language, and I am convinced that the absolutism of her position here is the heart of her artistic failure. In order to realize more explic-

[8] *Ibid.*, 192.

[9] Julian Sawyer, *Gertrude Stein: A Bibliography*, 30.

[10] *Ibid.*

itly the source of these characteristics, let us turn to a selection from *The Making of Americans:*

To be using a new word in my writing is to me a very difficult thing. Every word I am ever using in writing has for me very existing being. Using a word I have not yet been using in my writing is to me very difficult and a peculiar feeling. . . . I may know very well the meaning of a word and yet it has not for me weight and form and completely existing being. There are only a few words and with these mostly always I am writing that have for me completely entirely existing being, in talking I use many more of them of words I am not living but talking is another thing . . . often then I am using many words I never could be using in writing. In writing a word must be for me really an existing thing, it has a place for me as living, this is the way I feel about me writing.[11]

Although the full perverseness of Miss Stein's principle of selection is difficult for one to believe, it is at last fairly clear. She will use those words, and only those words, that set up in her the vibrations that convince her they are alive. That this is an impoverished language, that it is private, and that it is distinct from the language of human speech, all are inescapable conclusions.

Turning now to Gertrude Stein's idea of the proper place of beauty, specifically the beauty of sound, in language, we come to one of the commonest misconceptions

[11] Stein, *The Making of Americans,* 306.

about her work. It is widely assumed that Miss Stein was interested predominantly in the sound of her writing, that she was practicing an abstract art vaguely comparable to music. This is mere superstition, even though anyone unacquainted with her aesthetic credo arrives rather logically at this impression. If a work is logically unintelligible and if it pursues no typographical picture-drawing in the manner of, say, George Herbert or Cummings or modern advertising, it is indeed natural to assume that she is trying to make sounds that are beautiful, sounds that are in some sense musically meaningful; or even that she is after a kind of colossally elaborated onomatopoeia. However, this is not her aim, and another of the avenues by which one had hoped she would become intelligible comes to a dead end.

Anyone who reads much of Gertrude Stein's work aloud will very quickly conclude that it has little beauty and very rarely any abstract "meaning" as sound. It is very significant, too, that Miss Stein seldom read her own works aloud; in fact, she had never done so until her American lecture tour in 1934–35.[12] In this refusal she is still being consistent with the general line of her aesthetics, for she had a very deep-rooted mistrust of spoken literature. Writing designed to be heard is clearly writing designed for an audience, and the writer cannot possibly create it in the perfect state of unconsciousness of self and time.

Once again, this is not to say that she abhorred beauty of sound, but it is distinctly to say that she did not seek it. If it came, well and good; if it did not, she did not

[12] Stein, *Everybody's Autobiography*, 273.

mourn the fact. And when she became aware of it in her own writing process, she put it resolutely behind her. For a brief period about 1912, Miss Stein did allow herself the

luxury of melody, and only of the pieces written at this time may it be justly said that they move basically and intentionally by sound:

In doing these things I found I created a melody of words that filled me with a melody that gradually made me do the portraits easily by feeling the melody of anyone. And this began to bother me because perhaps I was getting drunk with melody and I do not like to be drunk I like to be sober and so I began again.[13]

Finally, she worked her way back to the only position in which she was comfortable in her sobriety: ". . . melody, beauty if you like was once more as it should always be a by-product."[14]

No, the absolute *gravitas* of Gertrude Stein's aesthetics is unmistakable. She was no Dionysiac. She noted approvingly to Virgil Thompson that "the Catholic Church makes a very sharp distinction between a hysteric and a saint."[15] It would be comforting to be able to feel that Miss Stein was hysteric, at least to the extent of appealing to our ears or to our buried associations. But this happens not to be true; to the end of her life she was

[13] Stein, "Portraits and Repetition," in *Lectures in America*, 199.
[14] *Ibid.*, 201.
[15] Stein, *The Autobiography of Alice B. Toklas*, 188.

uniformly "saintly" and exact in her pursuit of her very personal brand of "exactitude."

Gertrude Stein's theories on punctuation are part
133 of the whole language problem, and in explicating her attitude she is bright and interesting, always perfectly consistent within her eccentricity. Since the picture is in essence very simple, I shall discuss it as briefly as possible. Miss Stein is naturally concerned with making punctuation serve her generic ends of "presentness," the uniqueness of the artist's personal vision, and the sense of what were for her the proper ways for prose to move. Her general attitude toward punctuation can be made clear with one quotation from her lecture, "Poetry and Grammar"; the important subsidiary aspects can then be examined one at a time:

When I first began writing, I felt that writing should go on, I still do feel that it should go on but when I first began writing I was completely possessed by the necessity that writing should go on and if writing should go on what had colons and semi-colons to do with it, what had commas to do with it, what had periods . . . what had small letters and capitals to do with it.[16]

Her primary objection to conventional punctuation, then, was an unoriginal one: it interrupts the flow of prose.

Quotation marks, question marks, and exclamation marks she finds "unnecessary" because the job they

[16] Gertrude Stein, "Poetry and Grammar," in *Lectures in America,* 217.

are intended to do has already been accomplished by the logic of the context. Periods she always accepted because she "liked the look" of them and because the stopping they made was merely the record of the fact that sometimes one inevitably stopped. Necessity here, if not a virtue, is at least that necessity which she very occasionally admitted. "Beside that periods might later come to have a life of their own to commence breaking up things in arbitrary ways."[17] This notion gives rise to one of her more simple-minded stratagems for defeating the reader-enemy. For example, Parts II and III of "She Bowed to Her Brother," Miss Stein's record of her abstract consternation at having greeted her estranged brother, have an arbitrary period after every two or three words.[18]

Commas—and colons and semicolons, overgrown commas—receive her true sovereign contempt. These marks she found "servile" and their use "positively degrading." In denouncing them she is both eloquent and amusing:

> *Complications make eventually for simplicity. . . . Why if you want the pleasure of concentrating on the final simplicity of excessive complication would you want any artificial aid to bring about that simplicity.*[19]

A comma by helping you along holding your coat for

[17] *Ibid.*
[18] Gertrude Stein, "She Bowed to her Brother," in *Portraits and Prayers,* 237–40.
[19] Stein, "Poetry and Grammar," in *Lectures in America,* 220.

you and putting on your shoes keeps you from living your life as actively as you should lead it.[20]

135 *A long complicated sentence should force itself upon you, make you know yourself knowing it and . . . at the most a comma is a poor period that it lets you stop and take a breath but if you want to take a breath you ought to know yourself that you want to take a breath . . . you are always taking a breath and why emphasize one breath rather than another breath.*[21]

As always, there is much truth in what she says, but the final test of the value of the theory to the artist must rest with the work of art and with the matter to which vagaries of punctuation are applied. One can accept the eccentric punctuation of a Joyce, or even of a Cummings, but in Gertrude Stein's prose one too often feels that it merely introduces one more irritant. It is obvious, in any case, that punctuation omitted is the simplest element in the flatness of her prose and that punctuation arbitrarily used is the simplest element in its studied disjointedness.

One regrets leaving this matter without having sampled Miss Stein's dissertation on the apostrophe,[22] but it is probably not worth the space. It is sufficient to note that it provides one of her most charming digressions

20 *Ibid.*
21 *Ibid.*, 221.
22 *Ibid.*, 216.

in the wide-eyed naïve manner—naïveté made philosophical and built into the masonry of her aesthetics.

To focus the discussion of Gertrude Stein's views on the relationship of prose and poetry and the relevance of those views to her use of language, I will quote from her answer to one of her hecklers. The passage will also serve to keep before us the truth that, when she chose, Miss Stein could be, as I have said, pungent, clear, and direct. She is talking about the logic of the famous phrase, "rose is a rose is a rose is a rose":

Now listen! Can't you see that when the language was new—as it was with Chaucer and Homer—the poet could use the name of a thing and the thing was really there? He could say "O moon," "O sea," "O love" and the moon and the sea and love were really there. And can't you see that after hundreds of years had gone by and thousands of poems had been written, he could call on those words and find that they were just wornout literary words? The excitingness of pure being had withdrawn from them; they were just rather stale literary words. Now the poet has to work in the excitingness of pure being; he has to get back that intensity into the language. We all know that it's hard to write poetry in a late age; and we know that you have to put some strangeness, something unexpected, into the structure of the sentence in order to bring back vitality to the noun. Now it's not enough to be bizarre; the strangeness in the sentence structure has to come from the poetic gift, too. That's why it's doubly hard

to be a poet in a late age. Now you all have seen hundreds of poems about roses and you know in your bones the rose is not there. . . . Now listen! I'm no fool. I know that in
 daily life we don't go around saying "is a . . . is a . . . is a. . . ." Yes, I'm no fool; but I think that in that line the rose is red for the first time in English poetry for a hundred years.[23]

Here it is embarrassing but apposite to note that Julian Sawyer saw a yellow rose.[24] To return to the matter at hand, it is important to say that Gertrude Stein's thinking about prose and poetry is very intricate, and once more it is probably wise to take cognizance at the outset of her final position. Her theory grew out of her reflections on the total problem of language, and it is related as well to her views on narrative and the drama. I have detailed her sweeping renunciation of narrative in prose, of the narrative element in plays, and her invention in both prose and drama of a kind of movement that would take the place of narrative progression. This new movement was not to be movement at all in any accepted, conventional sense, but movement sterilized and transfixed into a kind of stasis in which artist and audience were free to contemplate the ideal truth of the moment of insight. "The better the play the more static," she says, and then extends the idea: "When you get to that point there is no essential

23 Wilder, Introduction to *Four in America,* by Gertrude Stein, v–vi.
24 Sawyer, *op. cit.,* 16.

difference between prose and poetry."[25] The crux of the matter seems to lie in her belief that in the course of her writing she had reduced prose, poetry, and the drama all to the same basic position: all were now free to "describe" "the static thing," the "essence" of the subject as it presents itself to the "knowing" of the creative mind. She believed that this was the problem and the mode she bequeathed to the generation that followed her.

It is the language aspect of this theory that concerns us now, and we can center our examination around Gertrude Stein's conception of the functions of the various parts of speech. Nouns, and variations on the theme of nouns, are the heart of her theory. To begin with the positive face of the matter: "I recognize verbs and adverbs aided by prepositions and conjunctions with pronouns as possessing the whole of the active life of writing."[26] The virtue of these parts of speech is their capacity for inner vitality, for having "existing being," a life of their own, independent of conventional, expected, objective usage.

Nouns, on the other hand, do not possess this vitality. "A noun is a name of anything," and a noun has vitality only in the verbal act of naming; that is, in the first naming of the object and for a brief period thereafter. After that time it is incapable of a life of its own. To put the matter in familiar semantic terms, a noun is not the thing itself; it is the name or symbol of that thing.

[25] Stein, "How Writing Is Written," in *The Oxford Anthology of American Literature*, II, 1451.

[26] Stein, "Poetry and Grammar," in *Lectures in America*, 220.

The actuality of the object is not its name, but its intrinsic matter, its "essence," and the essence of objects for Gertrude Stein was "the thing moving inside them that made them them." Since the name is emphatically not this essence, it becomes downright false as the name of the truth of the object, "and therefore slowly if you feel what is inside that thing you do not call it by the name by which it is known."[27] Of course, many people have felt substantially this inadequacy in our language and have worked for precision, a better "synonymy of word and thing," usually by an elaboration of definition and metaphor. But theirs is not Miss Stein's solution. Characteristically, her revolution must be drastic, if not total. She set about eliminating nouns, the received names of things, first in her prose.

"In coming to avoid nouns a great deal happens and has happened,"[28] she says. Some of her devices for avoiding nouns have already been mentioned in another context; for example, her deliberate misuse of nouns and her use of them in strictly private connotations, representative only of her momentary sense of her object, such words "as often as not had nothing to do with what any words would do that described that thing." In search of the "sense of immediacy," of recording the dynamic "verb" state of her knowing, she also resorted now to manipulating grammatical constructions in arbitrary ways, by "living in adverbs in verbs in pronouns, in adverbial clauses

[27] *Ibid.*, 210.
[28] *Ibid.*, 228.

written or implied and in conjunctions."[29] Such familiar phrases as "one being listening talking" and "one being going on existing" exemplify her preoccupation with constructions that would replace the noun. The method reaches its extremity in *The Making of Americans*, particularly in a tremendous and terribly tiresome proliferation of the present participle. It is this technique that Conrad Aiken, with much justice, called "a direct and perhaps simple-minded assault upon presentness."[30] The trait is especially obtrusive in Gertrude Stein's early work, and it never entirely disappears.

Having stripped away as much as she could of the noun state of prose, Miss Stein turned to poetry. She found that poetry, once it had lost its early narrative element, which "for the purpose of poetry . . . has now for a long time not had anything to do with being there,"[31] was a thing inseparable from nouns; that in fact its nounness was its trade-mark: ". . . poetry is a state of knowing and feeling a name."[32]

> *When I said.*
> *A rose is a rose is a rose is a rose.*
> *. . . I made poetry and what did I do I caressed completely caressed and addressed a noun.*[33]

[29] *Ibid.*
[30] Conrad Aiken, "We Ask for Bread," *New Republic*, Vol. LXXVIII, (April 4, 1934), 219.
[31] Stein, "Poetry and Grammar," in *Lectures in America*, 232.
[32] *Ibid.*, 233.
[33] *Ibid.*, 231.

Poetry, more slowly but just as definitely, comes to suffer from the same disability as prose. As she puts it in the long quotation with which I introduced this discussion, "the excitingness of pure being" has gone out of its nouns. It is therefore "doubly hard to be a poet in a late age." Of course, Miss Stein had hold here of an obvious but important truth: the "strangeness, something unexpected" of a Hopkins, a Yeats, a Dylan Thomas, or any sensitive poet in a late age reveals the search for renewed vitality in a language that has been abused by lesser talents. Although Gertrude Stein could see truth in theory, or even in the practice of others, in her own practice she emasculated truth by refusing to admit degree.

The term "poetry," like the term "play," has very little real meaning when applied by Miss Stein to her own work. Practically, her writing is poetry if it is not prose, and it is most difficult to make the distinction any more intelligible to a reader than that. Her "poems" conform to nothing one thinks of as poetry. The lines (what else can one call them?) of *Tender Buttons* are poetry to her. For this reason her poetic solution of the problem of bringing vitality back to the noun is practically indistinguishable from her prose solution. Actually the distinction is of little consequence, for both the motive and the result are the same in the two. First, she wondered, "Was there not a way of naming things that would not invent names, but mean names without naming them."[34] Then she applied her technique of concentrated, disciplined

[34] *Ibid.*, 236.

meditation until the essence of the object, the "existing so intensely" that was its true character, emerged, not in the form of a name, but as "the thing itself."[35] The language which was then the "poem" was the same kind of language which made her prose—the same idiosyncratic vocabulary, punctuation, and grammatical constructions—but Gertrude Stein felt that she had finally succeeded in lifting the dead hand of the noun from both poetry and prose.

The last portion of Miss Stein's theory of language, the ultimate relationship of prose and poetry, remains almost impenetrable as she herself has put it. However, it seems to resolve itself in this manner: Nouns, as names of things, have been replaced in poetry by "the thing itself" and by the essence of things. The replacement is static and descriptive, but, because of its native closeness to truth, uniquely accurate in descriptive power. Miss Stein concluded that it would become the function of this kind of poetry to deal with "everything that is not movement in space."[36] By this last category she means, strangely enough, narrative. Narrative for her does not involve movement in space because its essence is not physical progression; its essence is its truth or meaning, "the thing that makes what happens be what it is." This, too, is static and requires only description, and for this task the new, uniquely accurate "poetry" is best fitted.

The noun has been replaced in prose by language that is active in all the ways mentioned in this discussion,

[35] *Ibid.*, 245. [36] *Ibid.*

and it therefore moves. To the extent that prose is capable of movement or is dynamic in any sense, the noun is improper to narrative, the essence of which is not movement but stasis.

The movement Gertrude Stein saw as ultimately proper to prose in our time was either movement within, really a subjectively apprehended "vitality," or that discontinuous, directionless movement which is a negation of movement as progress; both of these alternatives amount, practically, to stasis. Since both are effectually static, prose and poetry are virtually one thing, and the distinction between them becomes academic. In her view of them, they solidified into one thing, which she saw as the new literary "form" she wished to bequeath to those who followed her:

> *This is essentially the problem with which your generation will have to wrestle. The thing has got to the point where poetry and prose have got to concern themselves with the static thing.*[37]

Having concluded that this was to be the new literary dilemma, Gertrude Stein not only laid it before others, but characteristically took its burden upon herself. *Four in America* is a pursuit of "the static thing." She tells us that in this work she was trying "to find out just what it is that what happens has to do with what is."[38]

[37] Stein, "How Writing Is Written," in *The Oxford Anthology of American Literature,* II, 1451.
[38] Stein, "Portraits and Repetition," in *Lectures in America,* 206.

Miss Stein's ruminations on prose and poetry, which becomes so abstruse that I cannot expound them with any great confidence, even after a too long steeping in them, show the ultimate abstraction of her aesthetics and her art and, I fear, their ultimate absurdity. She had moved farther and farther from the reader in order to follow her thought and art, by a process of steady narrowing and subtraction, to the point where very little remained: the static truth of the artist's moment of abstracted perception of reality was to be recorded in the stasis of his private language.

What is the artistic residue that can be transferred to a mind outside the artist? Tremendously interesting as theory, often as ideal, as art the remnant seems almost perfectly opaque. Just about everything communicable has been subtracted. It is still faintly possible that such an "essence" as Gertrude Stein's ideal static truth is communicable, but it seems certain to me that it must occur in an elaboration and refinement of the language as we know it or in the use of every possible resource of explanation and definition, illustration and example, logical correlation, metaphor, and symbol; in other words, it must occur in a method that is opposite that of Gertrude Stein.

It cannot, I think, be achieved by treating language as if it were not language, which is the way Miss Stein treats it. That is, she was so successful in abstracting her vision that she was able to forget the essentially symbolic character of words and the fact that a word points to a referent, the percept or concept which necessitated the invention of a symbol to express it in the first place. Having divorced a word from its ordinary referent in the process of her meditation, she felt free to apply it to a new idiosyncratic referent; the word could now symbolize anything she chose, and its new symbolism lay in her private state of mind, her momentary sense of its current "meaning." The great difficulty in communication comes from the very clear fact that the reader has not participated in the shift that moved the word from its old to its new symbolism; as a rule, what is clear to Gertrude Stein is not clear to him. What she is doing, it seems to me, is this: she is trying to handle words as if they were the essentially empty counters of music and painting. But words are not as empty or as malleable as sound or color or line; they are full and stiff, and if we want to manipulate them and still communicate the result, we have to keep the terms of the manipulation clear.

Miss Stein, as I must keep saying, was ruthlessly logical within the eccentricity of her aesthetics. She did not balk at the arid cul-de-sac of an art that conceived the ordinary reader as an enemy. If the reader is your enemy and you have to remain a worker in words, you circumvent your reader-enemy by inventing a language that is beyond him. Thus in vast areas of her writing, the areas that are most truly hers, Gertrude Stein is writing a language for which she has the only lexicon. Nothing else could show more clearly the fatal alienation of art from life in her aesthetics.

In *Everybody's Autobiography,* Miss Stein tells the story of a luncheon at Berkeley during which she was asked why she did not "write as she talked." Her reply was to ask her questioners whether, if they had invited Keats to lunch and asked him a question, they would expect him to answer with his "Ode to a Nightingale."[39] *Touché!* But surely the matter is one of degree. Most certainly the language of Keats' ode is not the language of his everyday discourse, but the difference between Keats' speech and his ode is simply not comparable in degree to the difference between Miss Stein's speech and the language of *Tender Buttons,* for example, or of *Geography and Plays.* The point to be made here is one Miss Stein has already suggested in her witticism. She worked concentratedly and philosophically at perfecting not only a separation but a divorce between literary language and the language of human correspondence; it was to be a separation that would move beyond degree to become one of kind.

Gertrude Stein actually looked with envy at those eras, which she saw as golden, when the language of literature was unintelligible outside the circle of the elect. One could dismiss such an attitude as mere snobbery, but the issue is more complicated than that and her position a trifle more respectable. Miss Stein was more blind than snobbish. She was simply committed philosophically to the doctrine that the creative state is inevitably and desirably unique; when it attempts to become a part of

[39] Stein, *Everybody's Autobiography,* 292.

"daily living," it destroys its uniqueness and, consequently, its validity.

Gertrude Stein details the separation of writing and speech at many points in her work, and we should look at some of her clearer statements because this separation is fundamental to the most obstinate tendency of her art and aesthetics. The outlines of her theory are contained in this passage from *Everybody's Autobiography*:

> *When I write I write and when I talk I talk and the two are not one . . . and when they come near being one then the inside is not inside and the outside is not outside and I like the inside to be inside and the outside to be outside, it makes it more necessary to be one.*[40]

To elucidate, the "inside" is the true reality, the essence as realized by the artist in the state of creativity; the "outside" is the apparent but false reality, the subject as seen in the deceptive clothing of objective externality. When the creative state is confused with the state of "daily living," truth and falsehood mingle and destroy the artist's knowing. "To be one" is Miss Stein's old concept of "entity" or "human mind."

It is perfectly fair to say that Miss Stein's thinking adds up to the conviction that art and life must be kept apart. Her most interesting defense of this indefensible position is contained in her essay, "An American and France"; there it becomes the rationale of her long ex-

40 *Ibid.*, 264.

patriation, indeed, of her whole way of life. "America is my country and Paris is my home town,"[41] she says. "I am an American and I have lived half my life in Paris, not the half that made me but the half in which I made what I made."[42] Thus she underlines a fundamental and highly conscious dichotomy. She explains her expatriation as a thing sought after and desirable, in fact necessary to art:

It is very natural that everyone who makes anything inside in themselves that is makes it entirely out of what is in them does naturally have to have two civilizations.[43]

. . . if you are you in your own civilization you are apt to mix yourself up too much with your own civilization.[44]

. . . the writer could not write unless he had the two civilizations coming together the one he was and the other that was there outside him and creation is the opposition of one of them to the other.[45]

One should bear no grudge against expatriates or expatriation, and to damn Gertrude Stein because she lived apart from her native land, as some have done, is sophomoric. But an ivory tower is an ivory tower, wherever its seat. The resoluteness with which Miss Stein opposed her Americanism to her long life in France is surely highly

[41] Stein, "An American and France," in *What Are Masterpieces,* 61.
[42] *Ibid.,* 62.
[43] *Ibid.*
[44] *Ibid.,* 63.
[45] *Ibid.,* 65.

symptomatic here. She conceived her life abroad not as an opportunity for merging with and assimilating a thing new and fine, but as a chance for the perfect condition of
 artistic isolation. She made no attempt to master the French language; she read it badly and infrequently and spoke it imperfectly—for forty-five years. She reveled in the luxury of what she saw as creative isolation, left "intensely alone with my eyes and my english."[46]

The record of Miss Stein's belief and practice is clear. The material of art occurs not in life but in the "knowing" of the hermetic artist; art is made "entirely out of what is in them." In the ideal creative state the artist not only separates the "inside" and the "outside," but also opposes them: "creation is the opposition of one of them to the other." Life is your enemy, the reader is your enemy; you circumvent both by spinning around yourself an impenetrable cocoon of abstraction, emerging periodically to mumble in a language known only to you. Art as a bilateral thing, a thing involving communication, or a giver and a receiver is dead, both by definition and by practice. Art by subtraction subtracts, finally, art itself.

[46] Stein, *The Autobiography of Alice B. Toklas*, 58.

8

RELATIONS TO THE ARTS:

I Like to Look at It

We have not finished examining the aesthetic position of Gertrude Stein until we explore her relationship to the arts in general—music and, especially, painting and literature. When the pattern is assembled on the basis of her published writings, it is oddly incoherent and not very impressive. Gertrude Stein lived a life completely bound up with the arts, but it is hard to persuade oneself that she penetrated them very deeply. Since it is impossible to do justice to these problems within the scope of this study, my comments must remain brief and speculative. The complicated subject of Miss Stein's place in the history of twentieth-century painting, for example, needs a book, and probably will someday receive one; the definitive researches for it would have to be made in Paris. However, we are certainly justified in coming to some independent conclusions on the evidence of her own statements.

The role of music, the simplest part of the problem, can be disposed of rather quickly. As I noted earlier, one of the most popular and understandable misconceptions about Miss Stein's writing is the belief that its appeal is primarily musical, to the ear. As recently as 1949, musician Leonard Bernstein could write:

> *Words are fundamentally conceptual and* transparent *(that is, they allow the idea to show through without interference) and are only* secondarily *decorative; while music is basically abstract and opaque, made up of notes which have no conceptual meaning in themselves, and acquire meaning only in relation to one another . . . it takes a Stein to musicalize words as successfully as she has.*
>
> *Stein has come closer than any other writer except Joyce to the medium of music.*[1]

Now this analysis proceeds on a logical assumption, for it is indeed startling that Gertrude Stein did not arrive at this position. The truth is that she never intended her words to have the complete "abstract and opaque" value of musical notes. She always stubbornly held that her words were "conceptual" and that their meaning was self-contained and available to anyone who was capable of making the leap up to Parnassus with her. It may appear that in so saying I am refuting the argument of my previous chapter, but I think not. It is true, as I said there,

[1] Leonard Bernstein, "Music and Miss Stein," *New York Times Book Review,* May 22, 1949, pp. 4, 22.

that she tended to handle words as one might handle essentially empty counters of music or painting; that is, she shifted them at will, with no sense of responsibility to "normal" syntax or context or reference. What she forgot was that her audience had not followed the shift in her meditation of the word to the new referent, and so she was always mystified at her failure to communicate. If Gertrude Stein "musicalizes" language, as Bernstein thought, she does so quite unconsciously. Nor did she want her words to have the sound of musical notes; as we have already seen, words as melody made her uncomfortable because they destroyed her "sobriety." To be sure, Bernstein's theory has real meaning when applied to Joyce, but Joyce was both a better musician and a better writer than Gertrude Stein.

Earlier, Paul Rosenfeld had held, in an analogy to music, that

> *For their veritable messages, the stories* [Three Lives] *and most of the novel* [The Making of Americans] *rely upon their slow oppositions of states of being built up voluminously by prose, their slow columinations and the effects of the slight variations in the oft-repeated vocabularies.*[2]

This is possibly a more tenable judgment, but it requires so many qualifications that, practically, it carries no great importance. It applies, in the first place, only to a com-

[2] Paul Rosenfeld, "The Place of Gertrude Stein," in *By Way of Art*, 120.

paratively small proportion of Miss Stein's work, her first two books; and it is not really true that the "veritable messages" of *Three Lives* are contained in its rhythm, although rhythm is extremely important, particularly in "Melanctha." The "message" of *Three Lives* is much more heavily conceptual than rhythmical and clearly discoverable intellectually in its language. Mr. Rosenfeld's opinion is more enlightening in the case of *The Making of Americans.* The essence of that book is its rhythm, and most of the power it commands of moving and even of instructing a reader lies in one's awareness of its vast structure as musically conceived. Rosenfeld's analogy, however, applies to structure alone and not to sound, and the structure of *The Making of Americans* is as much mathematical as it is specifically musical. Musical structure conceived as mathematics remains palatable to Gertrude Stein, and indeed she quotes with evident pleasure the analogy drawn by a French critic, Marcel Brion, between her grammatical structure and the structure of a Bach fugue.[3]

We must keep in mind that Miss Stein was concerned with exactitude and integrity, and in the pursuit of these ideals she believed the eye trustworthy and the ear traitorous. Therefore, we cannot, in good conscience, expect any real kinship to music.

Thornton Wilder credits her with having passed through a period when she was "a passionate and informed music lover,"[4] but his tribute is not in complete harmony

[3] Stein, *The Autobiography of Alice B. Toklas,* 42.
[4] Wilder, Introduction to *Four in America,* by Gertrude Stein, xxi.

with her own statements. At one point she writes: "... not that she ever cared for music naturally not."[5] "Music she only cared for during her adolescence. She finds it difficult to listen to it, it does not hold her attention,"[6] she says in *The Autobiography of Alice B. Toklas*.

In the long run, idiosyncrasy, as usual, provides the key. In a delightful bit from *Everybody's Autobiography*, Miss Stein paints a miniature of the mere idiosyncrasy that characterizes many of her reactions to the arts. It is astonishing to see how fatally much of Gertrude Stein is contained in this vignette (she speaks here of her practice in improvising on the piano):

... you never want to use anything but white keys black keys are too harmonious and you never want to do a chord chords are too emotional, you want to use white keys and play two hands together but not bother which direction either hand takes not at all you want to make it like a design and always looking and you will have a good time.[7]

Music, at any rate, "did not hold her attention," and this, too, is suggestive of a fact we cannot justly ignore. Many of Gertrude Stein's judgments in the arts are just as shallow and perverse as this one—which, it will be noted, is the familiar one of the college freshman: "The book held my attention to the very end." By no means

[5] Stein, *Everybody's Autobiography*, 139.
[6] Stein, *The Autobiography of Alice B. Toklas*, 62.
[7] Stein, *Everybody's Autobiography*, 229.

are all of Miss Stein's critical decisions so thin and cavalier, but a disturbing percentage of them are, and serious doubts are thereby cast on the quality of her intellectual involvement in the arts of her time.

When we turn from music to literature, we find a picture that is somewhat different but still basically simple. The question of literary "influence" upon Miss Stein's writing has little significance. Gertrude Stein is free of literary influence to a degree that has scarcely been true of any other writer since Homer. With the exception of *Three Lives*, her writing seems entirely *sui generis*. One must find a great deal of irony and pathos in the fact that her best book is her only unoriginal one. But in her characteristic independence, Miss Stein only proves herself consistent with her theory; in the terms of her aesthetics, as we have seen, the true artist is by definition separated from his predecessors. If he is not, he is a "minor person," an anachronism, not "contemporaneous." Therefore, as she developed her theory, she worked pointedly at taking her departure from a position at which no one else had arrived.

Gertrude Stein was far from being ignorant of literature. She was, as I have said, enormously literate. Her reading life, however, followed what is surely one of the strangest patterns ever assumed by a mind so ingestive and intelligent. She read, she tells us, "everything that was printed that came her way and a great deal came her way."[8] It seems almost literally true that she read "all of English literature" and reread much of it many times. She claims

[8] Stein, *The Autobiography of Alice B. Toklas*, 62.

that by the age of eight she had read all of Shakespeare and was trying to write plays in imitation of him. One of the many hilarious anecdotes of *The Autobiography of Alice B. Toklas* tells of her first attempt at a Shakespearean play; she got as far as a stage direction, "courtiers making witty remarks," but then she could think of no witty remarks and so had to abandon the project.[9] Her brother Leo says that she was fourteen when this phenomenon occurred;[10] whichever is true, the record is impressive. By the time of adolescence she was seriously bothered by the fear that there would soon be nothing left to read.

In later years her reading became almost unbelievably unselective. She read with apparently equal tolerance anything that fell under her eye; detective stories became a great passion; Wild West stories were completely absorbing. Thornton Wilder tells the story of her buying the seventy-year-old library of the Church of England at Aix-les-Bains:

They included some thirty minor English novels of the 'seventies, the stately lives of colonial governors, the lives of missionaries. She read them all. Any written thing had become sheer phenomenon; for the purposes of her reflections absence of quality was as instructive as quality.[11]

In all fairness, however, we should include Wilder's

[9] *Ibid.*, 62–63.
[10] Leo Stein, *op. cit.*, 190.
[11] Wilder, Introduction to *Four in America*, by Gertrude Stein, x.

next sentence: "Quality was sufficiently supplied by Shakespeare whose works lay often at her hand." The curious and surely symptomatic thing here is that Shakespeare and Wild West could coexist in Gertrude Stein's mind. We have here one of the most interesting examples of her refusal to make distinctions, which seems, when fully documented in other areas of her thinking, to be wholly characteristic and almost pathological. This is one of the phenomena that led to my earlier remark that Miss Stein's mind had become oddly fixed at the laboratory-observation level of "science" and that this was, unfortunately, the definitive result of her association with William James. Hers was an ignoble borrowing from a noble mind. The tendency for experience to become "sheer phenomenon" to Gertrude Stein is at once very revealing and very damaging. I shall investigate this quirk further later on; for now it is sufficient to make this point: the tendency for art to become "sheer phenomenon" often meant that Miss Stein's judgments in the arts amounted to nothing more important critically than giving voice to simple perverseness and dilettantism.

Among the serious portions of English literature her preferences were sound: Shakespeare, Fielding, Swift, Defoe, Jane Austen, and Trollope. In American literature her highest admiration went to Henry James. She felt that James was the one writer who had intimations of the direction in which she would take writing in the twentieth century: ". . . he being the only nineteenth century writer who being an american felt the method of the twentieth century."[12] She came to read James only in later life, however, and he can be claimed no more than any other author as a progenitor of her writing.

The only work for which a literary "influence" is clearly—or even unclearly—present is *Three Lives*, written before Gertrude Stein became Gertrude Stein. She tells us that she wrote the book in the presence of her translation, as an "exercise in literature," of Flaubert's *Trois Contes* and of a Cézanne portrait of a woman. The derivation of her title is obvious, and Flaubert's simplicity of style and his sympathy for his characters were doubtless of weight in Miss Stein's approach to her first writing. She departs radically from Flaubert, however, in observing from within the minds of her people and in beginning her technique of rhythmic repetitiveness. It may be that Flaubert's contribution was finally no more than a suggestion of the possibility that she could write and a suggestion of the kind of character that she could imitate from her own experience. The question is really unanswerable and of temporary importance, for Gertrude Stein rapidly sloughed off her best but most derivative manner.

Influence in the other direction, the influence of Gertrude Stein upon the writing of this century, is another subject about which there has been a great deal of extravagant talk. The truth is extremely difficult to determine. "Influence," one of the prime imponderables in literature, is particularly complicated in the case of Gertrude Stein. On the one hand we have the fact of the still-

[12] Stein, *The Autobiography of Alice B. Toklas*, 65.

born privateness of her own esoteric art; on the other, the enormous force of her personality and the undoubted fact that she came to know, in varying degrees of intimacy, virtually every American writer who rose to prominence between the great wars. *The Autobiography of Alice B. Toklas* presents Gertrude Stein as a kind of prophetess waited upon by a stream of fumbling seekers after light.

She was undoubtedly visited by the seekers, but what did they carry away? Miss Stein named the Lost Generation; did she also form it? It is a commonplace of literary historians to hold that she was fundamental to the development of Ernest Hemingway, Sherwood Anderson, and Thornton Wilder. Her influence has been claimed in the work of Eugene O'Neill, Carl Van Vechten, Erskine Caldwell, and William Faulkner—in the work of virtually every American writer of the interwar generation who seemed to belong to this century. One brave young man has even ventured that she left a visible mark upon T. S. Eliot.[13] However, there seems to be a lot of nonsense in all this. The literary tendencies often attributed to Gertrude Stein—the interest in "primitivism," in concision and precision, and in exploiting the colloquial aspects of life and language—were already at work in our literature and would have matured without her. They certainly entered the American graphic arts without her influence. Traces of all these movements can be found, strongly placed, in positions isolated from that of Gertrude Stein; they can be found, to name only the most obvious,

[13] W. H. Gardner, *Gerard Manley Hopkins,* 269.

in the works of Mark Twain, Walt Whitman, Stephen Crane, and Theodore Dreiser, and in the paintings of Bingham, Bellows, and Eakins.

It is illogical, on the other hand, to maintain that Miss Stein left no impression on the writing of our time. I am suggesting only that her importance has been exaggerated. The truth seems to be that her real influence comes through Hemingway—through Hemingway's refinement and elaboration of techniques and attitudes that he learned in part from her. There can be no disputing the fact of their relationship. John Peale Bishop reports a conversation in which Hemingway said to him, in comparing the criticism he received from Ezra Pound and from Miss Stein, "Ezra was right half the time. . . . Gertrude was always right."[14] Some of the most interesting pages of *The Autobiography of Alice B. Toklas* are devoted to Miss Stein's association with Hemingway. We learn there, for example, that he copied for publication fifty pages of *The Making of Americans* and then read the proofs. Correcting proofs is, as Miss Toklas says, "like dusting, you learn the value of the thing as no reading suffices to teach it to you."[15] But Hemingway was too intelligent and much too "Rotarian," as Gertrude Stein put it, to take his lessons from that book. What he learned from Miss Stein, as Bishop conjectures, was the technique of repetition and the literary utility of the sentence struc-

[14] John Peale Bishop, "Homage to Hemingway," in *After the Genteel Tradition* (ed. by Malcolm Cowley), 193.

[15] Stein, *The Autobiography of Alice B. Toklas*, 179.

ture of ordinary American speech. Other than these details, she probably taught him something even more important, the ideal of literature as an enormously painstaking craft.

Hemingway grew away from her in a productive direction, one which amounted to a dilution of her teachings and a negation of her practice. He learned, among other things, to use Gertrude Stein's tools with flexibility and moderation and without monotony, things that her writing can teach no one. Gertrude Stein finally concluded that Hemingway "looks like a modern and he smells of the museums."[16] Ironically, however, Hemingway's vestigial museum quality has kept him readable, while Miss Stein's modernity has found no real audience. It is Hemingway's dilution of Gertrude Stein, I feel, that is her real force in literature. The only one of her texts that has marked the literary direction is the one in which she "smells of the museums." None of her more characteristic works has influenced any writer who has amounted to anything. There is irony and pathos in this, and there should have been instruction for Miss Stein. But to her it meant not that she was mistaken in her method, but that she was right in her assumption of superiority to the rabble of readers, and she went on storing up treasures in heaven, being doomed to poverty on earth.

The question of Gertrude Stein's relationship to painting is another thorny one. When the record is assembled, the final impression is not as complimentary to

[16] *Ibid.*

her as is commonly assumed. There is no doubt that she and Leo were among the very first to buy and display the works of the three most important modern painters, Cézanne, Matisse, and Picasso. But against this fact must be set still another: the first insight was Leo's, although she does her best to obscure this truth;[17] furthermore, Miss Stein's lecture on "Pictures" is the most appallingly empty thing she ever wrote in her communicative manner. The fundamental questions here are how thoroughly she understood painting as an art and to what extent the influence of painting is operative in her creative work. As in the case of her reading, one finds her to be a very nearly incredible combination of the initiate and the dilettante, the perceptive and the absurd. In the long run, the strongest impression is that of the inevitable idiosyncrasy, of judgments sometimes solidly founded, sometimes unbelievably perverse, antiartistic, and anti-intellectual.

We can trace Gertrude Stein's creative debt to painting in two main portions of her work: in *Three Lives* and in the period that runs roughly from 1910 to 1920. *Three Lives* was written, as we have noted, under the double influence of Flaubert and the Cézanne portrait. Although this sort of judgment is highly speculative, one would suspect that Cézanne suggested the technique of development by successive, articulated brush strokes, the use of strong, distinct color areas, and perhaps even the basic earthy, peasant conception of character. Again, much of this is in *Trois Contes,* and all of it was native to the people and the experience Miss Stein was recording.

Gertrude Stein says flatly at one point that her "middle writing was painting."[18] She apparently refers particularly to *Tender Buttons* and her early portraits.

She tells us, for example, that in *Tender Buttons* she "tried to include color and movement."[19] In these writings she seems to have attempted something very much like the practice of the cubist painters in their attempts to reduce form to its ultimate geometrical verities, searching for the reality that underlay surface structure and disposing these fragments on a surface often supplied with a single remnant of reality as conventionally viewed—a printed letter, a subway ticket, a musical symbol, a bit of glass—any piece of the false reality of surface. Miss Stein's own bent was always just this analytical and just this distrustful of "objective" reality. In the writings of this period, "objectivity" is supplied often only by the title of the work, by a date, or by a scrap of conversation; the rest is the probing, anatomical dismemberment into abstracted fragments of the artist's private vision.

Gertrude Stein's long, intimate association with Picasso is common knowledge. In *The Autobiography of Alice B. Toklas* his name appears more often than that of any other person except the heroine. Miss Stein gives this interesting, even moving, picture of them together:

They sit in two low chairs up in his apartment studio,

[17] Leo Stein, *op. cit.*, 148.

[18] Stein, *Everybody's Autobiography*, 180.

[19] Stein, "Portraits and Repetition," in *Lectures in America*, 189.

knee to knee and Picasso says, expliquez-moi cela. And they explain to each other. They talk . . . about pictures, about dogs, about death, about unhappiness.[20]

One wonders which partner contributed more. The account of their first meeting,[21] at which Gertrude Stein stole a piece of bread from Picasso, might easily be taken as symbolic of a great deal in their relationship. One finds ideas that were originally Picasso's cropping up periodically as Gertrude Stein's own creation. The doctrine of the necessary ugliness of fundamentally original art, for example, which Miss Stein often passes off as her own, belongs, in reality, to Picasso.

A few other items should be noted. The first purchases of the bold new paintings were the result of Leo's insight, not Gertrude's; this we have remarked. Then there is the very damaging fact that a group of the people mentioned in *The Autobiography of Alice B. Toklas*—Matisse, Braque, Tristan Tzara, André Salmon, Eugene and Maria Jolas—felt strongly enough about what they saw as fundamental inaccuracies and insensitivity in Miss Stein's account of her time to issue a "Testimony Against Gertrude Stein" as a separate pamphlet-number of *transition.* They not only impugn her accuracy; they picture her as personally incapable of any real penetration of the arts of her time. The following excerpts typify these resonantly peevish denunciations:

[20] Stein, *The Autobiography of Alice B. Toklas,* 64.
[21] *Ibid.,* 38.

MATISSE: *Gertrude Stein has contacted indiscriminately things about which, it seems to me, she has understood nothing.*[22]

MARIA JOLAS: . . . *she would eventually tolerate no relationship that did not bring with it adulation.*[23]

BRAQUE: *Miss Stein understood nothing of what went on around her.*[24]

SALMON: . . . *what confusion! What incomprehension of an epoch!*[25]

Even if one arbitrarily discounts such statements by half on the grounds that they are made in personal rancor, serious shadows are thrown on the picture of Gertrude Stein as the high priestess of modern art. Leo Stein supports the above condemnations at every point.[26]

The truth seems to be that Gertrude Stein, in painting, was neither a charlatan nor a seer. She was a woman of vast experience and great intelligence whose judgments were weirdly bent by an idiosyncratic vein that split her perceptions from top to bottom. She is capable of cavalier dismissals that banish tremendous areas from her ken. "El Greco meant a great deal to me once and now I would not go anywhere to look at them."[27] Because neither sculp-

[22] Henri Matisse, "Testimony Against Gertrude Stein," 7.
[23] Maria Jolas, "Testimony Against Gertrude Stein," 12.
[24] Georges Braque, "Testimony Against Gertrude Stein," 13.
[25] André Salmon, "Testimony Against Gertrude Stein," 15.
[26] Leo Stein, *op. cit.*, 134–37, 141–42, 148–49, 152, 154–55.
[27] Stein, *Everybody's Autobiography*, 131.

ture nor water colors "hold her attention," they are worthless, and so on.

Her American lecture on "Pictures" contains very little that strikes one with any force, but it does show very interestingly the pervasiveness in her thinking of two of the eccentricities we have already noted: her fondness for flatness and the strange absence of discrimination. Thornton Wilder could say of her reading, "Any written thing had become sheer phenomenon; for the purposes of her reflections absence of quality was as instructive as quality";[28] and the same could be said, with much justice, of Miss Stein's reactions to painting. At the beginning of this lecture she tells unblushingly of her answer to a question put by the *Little Review*: "What do you feel about modern art?" Her answer was: "I like to look at it."[29] Now the whole of Gertrude Stein's appreciation of painting is not as simple minded as this statement might lead one to believe, but a good deal of it is. Witness the following passage from the lecture:

Once an oil painting is painted, painted on a flat surface, painted by anybody who likes or is hired or is interested to paint it, or who has or has not been taught to paint it, I can always look at it and it always holds my attention. The painting may be good it may be bad, medium or very bad or very good but anyway I like to look at it.[30]

[28] Wilder, Introduction to *Four in America*, by Gertrude Stein, x.
[29] Stein, "Pictures," in *Lectures in America*, 59.
[30] *Ibid.*, 61.

This passage does not, of course, imply that Gertrude Stein was incapable of discriminating among paintings, and it would be foolish, in the face of considerable

contrary evidence, to contend that it does. The really interesting thing is the evidence that she had trained herself to be discriminating or undiscriminating ad libitum, as it suited "the purposes of her reflection" of the moment. She was able, apparently, simply to suspend her critical faculty and to make of all art "sheer phenomenon." Nothing is more indicative of the whole direction of her aesthetics, indeed of her life.

Her insistence here on the flat surface with the minute degree of modeling, the *stiacciato* supplied by oil, relates itself conclusively to that general orientation to flatness in her literary point of observation that we saw earlier. Her practice, artistically, of the plane's-eye point of observation has become, by an interesting and perfectly consistent extension, a mainspring of her appreciative mechanisms as well.

The important thing to be learned from such a survey of Gertrude Stein's relationship to the arts is the true omnipresence of her eccentricity. She accepts, rejects, and modifies the arts wholly on the basis of a private value structure that often seems shallow, mistaken, or merely perverse; in any case, she was at great pains to maintain it uncorrupted by conventionality.

9

AN EVALUATION:

Think of Shakespeare and Think of Me

It would be a great deal easier to measure Gertrude Stein if she would let us alone. It would be much easier if she would let us weigh her as a minor writer rather than a major one, or as a scientist-philosopher rather than a creative artist, or as a follower of a bypath rather than of the highroad of literature. I am suggesting, obviously, that these alternatives seem to be the essential truths about her, but she will have none of them. The critic has to cut his way through a jungle of Miss Stein's ponderous pronouncements on the subject of herself, backed by all the weight of her full assurance and supported in some degree by the evidences of her wholly real independence and intelligence and the acclamation of eloquent and respectable friends.

Gertrude Stein's ego is one of the great egos of all time. It is monumental; it is heroic. Flat assertion of her own genius is a leitmotiv in virtually all her books. "Think of the Bible and Homer think of Shakespeare and think of me,"[1] she says; "I am one of the masters of English prose";[2] "In this epoch the only real literary thinking has been done by a woman";[3] "in english literature in her time she is the only one";[4] "I know that I am the most important writer writing today";[5] "I have been the creative literary mind of the century."[6] She makes Miss Toklas say: "The three geniuses of whom I wish to speak are Gertrude Stein, Pablo Picasso and Alfred Whitehead. . . . I have known only three first class geniuses and in each case on sight within me something rang."[7]

I am inclined to think she gave Miss Toklas only a two-thirds chance of being right. Of course, Gertrude Stein became accustomed to the kind of carping insensitivity I am according her here, and she took it as one of the unavoidable tribulations attendant on genius. "Naturally I have my detractors," she said to Wombley Bald. "What genius does not?"[8] It may be true indeed that Miss Stein needs to be seen as a genius to be seen at all. That is, we evaluate her as a being essentially not measurable at all, as apart, unique. When we try to fit her into a context involving normality or moderate supranormality, she does

[1] Stein, *The Geographical History of America*, 81.
[2] Stein, *Everybody's Autobiography*, 114.
[3] Stein, *The Geographical History of America*, 182.
[4] Stein, *The Autobiography of Alice B. Toklas*, 64.
[5] Stein, *Everybody's Autobiography*, 28.
[6] *Ibid.*, 23.
[7] Stein, *The Autobiography of Alice B. Toklas*, 5.
[8] Samuel Putnam, *Paris Was Our Mistress*, 137.

not fit; there is no common yardstick; the scales refuse to function. Perhaps we must agree with Julian Sawyer's judgment of her "absolute perspicacity." If she has that, she is beyond us; we cannot know her—and the critic's job is simplified into one of awe.

If Gertrude Stein is a genius, she is one in the vulgar sense of the term: perversely elevated, isolated, inhuman. Hers is not the friendly, communicative genius of her masters, James and Whitehead, or even Picasso, pulling us gently or roughly up to the heights of their new insight. She is a genius with a tragic flaw, one curiously like the old flaw of Oedipus and Lear—the fatal combination of pride and power and blindness. We must say this with the full knowledge that Gertrude Stein seemed all her life to be trying to communicate to us, that she worked with sweat and occasional humility to make us know her mind. That, however, is her colossal blindness and her arrogance; convinced of the absolute rightness of her vision and of her literary record of that insight, she refused all moderation or compromise.

It seems to me that Miss Stein is a vulgar genius talking to herself, and if she is talking to herself, she is not an artist. It is because she does talk to herself that she offers insuperable difficulties to both reader and critic. I suggest, therefore, that she be defined out of existence as an artist. To be an artist, she must talk to us, not to the dullest or the most tradition bound or the most unsympathetic of us, but to those of us who are flexible, those willing to be fruitfully led. There is not world enough or time enough for Gertrude Stein's kind of writing; too much in literature is both excellent and knowable.

What I am trying to say is that most of the confusion about Gertrude Stein seems the result of trying to understand her in a mistaken context. The original mistake is Miss Stein's; it happened when she defined herself as an artist, thereby obscuring from herself and her readers the fact that both her ends and her means pointed toward philosophy by way of science. The whole cast and capability of her mind was scientific, reflective, rational, philosophic. Of the truly creative ability to fabricate and counterfeit, to excite and to move and to instruct by fact or fiction conceived as dramatic, narrative, or lyric, she had only a rudimentary portion, and this she studiously suppressed until it was very nearly dead. Her works are not, properly speaking, art at all. Her aim was to "describe reality," but description alone is not art but science. In her aesthetics she reflects on reality as well, and it becomes philosophy.

Her "art" is one of subtraction and narrowing throughout. In her art she does not reflect, for reflection entails consciousness of identity and audience, an awareness fatal to the creative vision. She rules out the imagination because it is the hunting ground of secondary talent. She rules out logical, cause-effect relations: "Question and answer make you know time is existing." She rules out distinctions of right and wrong: "Write and right. Of course they have nothing to do with one another." She will have no distinctions of true and false: "The human mind is not concerned with being or not being true." She abjures beauty, emotion, association, analogy, illustration, metaphor. Art by subtraction finally subtracts art itself. What remains as the manner and matter of the specifically "creative" works of Gertrude Stein is the artist and an object vis-à-vis. This is not art; this is science. Miss Stein would turn the artist into a recording mechanism, a camera that somehow utters words rather than pictures.

It is vastly ironic that in a century in which the arts have been in pell-mell flight from the camera, she, who thought herself always galloping in the van of "contemporaneousness," has fled toward the camera. That hers is an eccentric camera, a literal camera obscura, does not make it less a camera. That in her early writing she was interested in what was under the surface, in the "inside," does not make her less a photographer. There she may be operating an X ray, but even its function is to take the picture, not to comment upon it, clothe it, or give it life in beauty or ugliness. Hers is still the "intellectual passion for exactitude in description."

Gertrude Stein's mistake, one must think, lies in conceiving as a sufficient ideal the thing William James handed her as a tool, the tool of rigidly objective scientific observation. She was conscious of this orientation toward science to some degree at one point in her work, *The Making of Americans;* after that she thought she had lost it and embarked upon a purely creative tack. But it seems that she never truly lost the scientific point of view. Whatever her subject, her "art" remained, within its idiosyncrasy, photographic in intention and in method.

Miss Stein makes a passing observation about painting in *The Autobiography of Alice B. Toklas* that is highly significant for an insight into her own work:

> *One of the things that always worries her about painting is the difficulty that the artist feels and which sends him to painting still lifes, that after all the human being essentially is not paintable . . . if you do not solve your painting problem in painting human beings you do not solve it at all.*[9]

Yet she "always made her chief study people."[10] Thus her chief study is people, who essentially are not paintable, and she is committed by the terms of her creed to painting them. One of the critical verities about Gertrude Stein is that she would never be instructed by impossibility, and one suspects that this particular impossibility is the focal dilemma of her work. It is her commitment to this impossibility, more than any of her ostensible dilemmas—the realization of "the complete actual present" or "the sense of immediacy" — that makes her twist and turn, that "made me try so many ways to tell my story" as she puts it.

True, "abjectly true," as William James would say, the human being is not paintable. Nor is he photographable; no matter whether one snaps his exterior or X-rays

[9] Stein, *The Autobiography of Alice B. Toklas*, 99.
[10] *Ibid.*

his bones and his liver and lights, one still does not have a human being. All great artists have recognized this abject truth; it is the reason they have set about apprehending the "poor, bare, forked animal"—still imperfectly, of course—by a means other than painting or by a means in addition to painting, by all the proliferation of the resources of language and thought and imagination they could command.

Gertrude Stein never effectively admitted that she could not paint or photograph man. She continued to try as long as she lived. And she, like the painters, was driven, in a very curious and retributively just way, into the retreat of still life. There was the difference, however, that the retreat became for her not occasional but chronic, not therapy but the disease itself. She retreated into the outright still life of the unpopulated *Tender Buttons,* or she sterilized and transfixed man until he was virtually a still-life element, no more humanly alive than Cézanne's apples or Braque's guitars. Why else should a play resemble a landscape, as she insists it should? In a very real sense, all the later works of Gertrude Stein, with the exception of those that are in some way autobiographical, are still lifes. To become an artist in the true sense of the word, Miss Stein would have had to surrender to the impossibility of apprehending man by unaided science.

It is significant, surely, that the one work of Gertrude Stein's with real artistic stature is the one that is least exclusively painterly. *Three Lives* is written as one feels, vaguely, a work of art should be written. It is written, that is, by a process of imagination applied to life experienced and directed by an informing philosophical theme and purpose; it is long and thoughtful in gestation; it envisions a reader to be enlightened and moved, and therefore it proceeds with a consciousness of form applied to part and whole, of language to be shaped and disciplined to delight and clarify. In a word, it is art achieved by the addition or multiplication of the tools of the writer. *Three Lives* was written, too, before experience became "sheer phenomenon" to Gertrude Stein, while she yet retained the desire to select and evaluate and be herself moved by her experience, before the encroachment of science upon her art imposed the necessity of removing herself emotionally from her subject and enjoined her to see mechanically rather than qualitatively.

The peripatetic origin of *Three Lives* reminds one of the method of the early Joyce, and indeed this book marks the one point in her work where one is moved to suspect that she, too, had within her the equipment of a first-rate creative writer. The book formed itself in her mind as she walked back and forth across Paris between her rue de Fleurus home and Picasso's Montmartre studio, where she was posing for the famous portrait now in the Museum of Modern Art. "Melanctha," the most famous of the three lives, combines bits picked up by her eyes and ears during the Paris walks, with people and incidents recollected from her experience, as a Johns Hopkins medical student, in delivering Negro babies in the slums of Baltimore. Another of the lives relates the story of a servant she had while a student in Baltimore. Such stories should have resulted from clear and close observations; they should be moving, and they are. As Edmund Wilson says, one feels Gertrude Stein living in the minds of these three simple-complex women, reproducing the movements of their consciousness with an identification that seems almost perfect.

For all its excellence, Miss Stein herself seems not to have regarded her *Three Lives* very highly, despite the fact that it gave her her widest literary influence and her soundest critical esteem. She mentions it comparatively seldom, usually as the product of an imperfect, formative period. She seems vaguely and illogically ashamed of the book. What really bothers her, of course, is that it retains likenesses to the writing of the past. In it, as she says, she was "groping" for her true direction. The fact that her groping was better literature than her fully formed method should have contained a lesson for her, but it did not. The very things that made the fineness of the book are the things she carefully cut away as her style matured—the sense of complete emotional and intellectual involvement and the full use of the writer's common tools of observation and re-creation in language. Ultimately the artist as a sensitized human being is replaced by the artist as a recorder; all that remains of the early multiplicity of resources is the emergent moments of "reality" as they move past the lens of the camera artist.

Three Lives, as I have said, stands as Miss Stein's point of closest identification with the mind of a character, and it provides us with an important observation on her relation to the contemporary "stream of consciousness" technique. It should be recalled here that it was her teacher, William James, who coined the term. In this book Gertrude Stein, whether or not she knew it, was creating in an approximation of this style. The symptomatic thing is that this is the only instance in which it is the mind of the character whose stream is followed. After this single experience Miss Stein retains the stream, but she shifts the focus to the writer, to the flow of her "knowing." In one more of the many ironies that crop up with Miss Stein as she moves toward science and objectivity and forgetfulness of self, she is turned in upon herself. She did not forget self, but she forgot nearly everything else and again trapped herself in the multiple paradox of her theory.

For all its unlikeness to her later writing, *Three Lives* contains in embryo two tendencies that later became very important, indicating the fundamental orientation of her art to science. For one thing, she adumbrates here her disposition to classify people by types that are vaguely psychological, the interest that was soon to become the whole of *The Making of Americans,* containing as it does the germ of the attitude that finally turned humanity into "sheer phenomenon" for her. For another, she begins her pursuit of a kind of language that will be for her the scientifically accurate re-creation of her subject. In *Three Lives,* language is still largely under control; straightforwardly conceptual and communicative, it keeps the reader in mind, intending to share with him a finely realized experience. The language in *Three Lives* is, in general, intellectually and dramatically and poetically satisfying. Only in "Melanctha" does one see it begin to slip out of her grasp and begin to control her. The repetitions and ramblings and rebeginnings continue to the point where it becomes obvious that Gertrude Stein is giving birth, right under our eyes, to her fatal habit of ignoring the inevitable gap between the sensibilities of writer and reader. Large portions of the latter half of "Melanctha" cross the border of enlightenment and interest into that limbo of dullness and torpor in which Miss Stein soon becomes entrenched.

She is beginning to lose her sense of proportion in the egoistic excitement of arriving at the state of ideal "creative recognition." The deadly folding-in upon self, the constricting of the field of vision and depth of purpose, the noxious linguistic idiosyncrasy—all get under way. In her first book Gertrude Stein has already begun to insulate herself from her reader, but the book remains a fine one because the process is as yet imperfect.

Miss Stein's second book, *The Making of Americans*, three years in the writing (1906–1908), was not published until 1925. It was this book that Conrad Aiken called a "fantastic disaster."[11] In it the movement away from art and toward science is far more complete than in the earlier work, and the effect is paralyzing indeed. But her aim in *The Making of Americans*, if not genuinely

[11] Aiken, "We Ask for Bread," *New Republic*, Vol. LXXVIII (April 4, 1934), 219.

artistic, is genuinely, if wrongheadedly, humane. The book grew out of her experiments at Radcliffe in "cultivated motor automatism," or automatic writing, with a large group of men and women students as her subjects. She found that her experiments proved nothing, but she conceived a profound interest in what she saw as the revelations of character inherent in the reactions of the individual students to the testing process, and when her study appeared in the *Psychological Review*, it was significantly subtitled "A Study of Character in Relation to Attention."[12] She had begun to see character revealed in every word and gesture, to see these symptoms grouping themselves into patterns indicative of basic personality types. When she came to the writing of *The Making of Americans,* which began as the history of her own family, she naturally found herself returning to this conception of human beings as types. Gertrude Stein then fantastically elaborated upon the purpose of the work until it came to be the history of "everyone who ever was or is or would be living."[13]

Her motive, we repeat, was still idealistic and humane:

> *I was sure that in a kind of a way the enigma of the universe could in this way be solved. That after all description is explanation, and if I went on and on and on enough*

[12] Gertrude Stein, "Cultivated Motor Automatism," *Psychological Review,* Vol. V (May, 1898), 295–306.
[13] Stein, "The Gradual Making of The Making of Americans," in *Selected Writings,* 215.

I could describe every individual human being that could possibly exist.[14]

Although this procedure promises little for the solution of the "enigma of the universe," it nevertheless suggests a great deal about the enigma of Gertrude Stein. Her first premise, that "description is explanation," gives prime evidence of the fixation of her mind at the shallow level of laboratory science. Miss Stein never really learned that describing human beings never explains them. The painters knew that the human being "essentially is not paintable," and she knew they knew it, but she did not know it herself. Her second premise, that it is possible by artful grouping to "describe every individual human being that could possibly exist," strikes one as equally invalid, testifying to the same disease indicated by her first error. Likeness among human beings is revealing to science, but the uniqueness of every human atom is the more profound truth and the thing that art most needs to concern itself with. The word "individual" is an anomaly as Gertrude Stein uses it. The individual is to her a classifiable phenomenon, hence not an individual at all. It is largely her mechanistic view of man that makes the "people" who inhabit her books after *Three Lives* seem so dun and protoplasmic.

At any rate, though her aim seems to be limited here by an extreme error in logic, it is interesting in that it marks almost the only point in her work where some-

[14] *Ibid.*

thing like a moral purpose is visible. Her method, on the other hand, is pure, if eccentric, science. The heart of her theory lay in the shaky and curiously shallow doctrine of "resemblances." She observed her associates closely and watched for "resemblances" in their minutest gestures, in their "expressions or turn of the face." Then she traced likenesses and differences in presumably deeper aspects of character until she arrived at the classification of the "individual."

The child Stephen Dedalus at Clongowes Wood College noticed with astonishment that "every single fellow had a different way of walking," but the mature Joyce did not consider this observation sufficiently meaningful evidence for the determination of character. It is unfair to say that Gertrude Stein found "expressions or turn of the face" sufficient data, but in truth, her penetration of character does not go impressively deep. For example, witness her ultimate categories of personality in *The Making of Americans*:

There are then always the two kinds in all who are or were or ever will have in them human being, there are then always to my thinking in all of them the two kinds of them the dependent independent, the independent dependent; the first have resisting as the fighting power in them, the second have attacking as their natural way of fighting.[15]

[15] Stein, *The Making of Americans*, 132–33.

Although this idea is vaguely promising, given elaboration and dramatization of the "kinds" through fully developed, interacting individuals, Miss Stein never really supplies the materials we need if the theory is to have life and meaning. But it does represent the ultimate in her realization of character in terms of personality types.

Scientifically enough, Gertrude Stein actually made enormous charts to record her researches into the "kinds" of human beings. In the process, people became for her the same kind of dun protoplasm they become for the reader when she transfers the results to the printed page:

> *I got to the place where I didn't know whether I knew people or not. I made so many charts that when I used to go down the streets of Paris I wondered whether they were people I knew or ones I didn't.*[16]

But she still refused to be instructed by impossibility, and she wrote her book.

In *The Making of Americans*, Miss Stein was really pursuing what she called the "bottom being" of individuals, a phase of personality interestingly close to that "essence" of people and objects that became her constant and increasingly esoteric preoccupation. Her method, which at first glance seems intuitive and inspirational, is in fact nothing of the kind. It is the geared, oiled functioning of the artist who has made himself as nearly as possible

[16] Stein, "How Writing Is Written," in *The Oxford Anthology of American Literature*, II, 1449.

a scientifically accurate recording mechanism. Edmund Wilson's metaphor describing Gertrude Stein as a kind of "august human seismograph"[17] is by no means inapt.

Miss Stein's apparatus includes a picture-taking eye, a sound-recording ear, and an occult attachment that "listens" seismically to the subtle vibrations of personality—all of it joining in the "listening to repeating" that constitutes the scientific apprehension of the "bottom being" of personality.

It is fascinating to watch the machine at work if one takes it in small, selective doses. One can feel the engine roar or falter or idle, according to the degrees of its current attainment, as it chugs along at the job of sorting and filing the punched and tabbed cards of categorized human beings:

Alfred Hersland then . . . was of the resisting kind of them in men and women and now then I will wait again and soon then I will be full up with him, I am now then not completely full up with him. Now I am again beginning waiting to be full up completely full up with him. I am very considerably full up now with the kind of being in him, I will be waiting and then I will be full up with all the being in him, that is certain, and so then now a little again once more then I am waiting waiting to be filled up full completely with him with all the being ever in him.[18]

[17] Wilson, *op. cit.*, 252–53.
[18] Stein, *The Making of Americans*, 291.

Here we are fully in the presence of that process that strips the flesh from bones and drains the blood from veins of the human beings who are currently Gertrude Stein's object. Her people, like Prufrock, end up "formulated, sprawling on a pin." In the process of Miss Stein's coming to know them "scientifically," they are robbed of life for the reader. The people of *The Making of Americans* are not alive as are those of *Three Lives*. They begin now to be the "sheer phenomena" they later become completely—objectively and also subjectively unrecognizable, quantitatively weighed and calipered.

Note again in the above quotation the tendency to focus attention on the mind of the writer. The stream of consciousness is the writer's stream; the human character is grist for his mill.

Gertrude Stein assures us that she worked "passionately and desperately"[19] on *The Making of Americans*, and there is no reason to doubt her. How pathetic that so much life went into the book and that so little comes out! The book that in its ideal and in its magnificent first pages promises so much becomes, in the process of scientific realization, phenomenally toneless and dull. Since the scientist can omit nothing, must record every instance of every "characteristic" gesture of "being," since he must record in chartable symbols, he passes on to us a record that is readable as any chart is readable, but that record is unreadable as art—hopeless, soporific, anesthetic. *The*

[19] Stein, "The Gradual Making of The Making of Americans," in *Selected Writings*, 215.

Making of Americans, one of the longest books ever written, must also be one of the dullest: flat, featureless, incredibly repetitious, deadly.

185 In classifying Gertrude Stein's writings, apart from *Three Lives,* which must always be set aside as her best and least characteristic work, we can group them roughly into three divisions. It may be argued that in so doing we are committing Miss Stein's own sin of "classification," but we can advance in defense the need for compression, plus the fact that in the books there is very little warm life to be injured. In the first group we have the books that are largely autobiographical: *The Autobiography of Alice B. Toklas, Everybody's Autobiography, Wars I Have Seen,* and *Paris, France.* In the second group, the mass of her specifically "creative" works: *The Making of Americans, Tender Buttons, Lucy Church Amiably, Matisse Picasso and Gertrude Stein, How to Write, The Geographical History of America or the Relation of Human Nature to the Human Mind, Ida, Four in America, Brewsie and Willie, Blood on the Dining Room Floor,* the "forgotten" book, *Things as They Are,* and the various omnibus volumes, *Geography and Plays, Useful Knowledge, Operas and Plays, Portraits and Prayers, Last Operas and Plays,* and the seven posthumous volumes. In the last group, Miss Stein's aesthetic and critical writings: *Lectures in America, Narration, Picasso,* and *What Are Masterpieces.*

The books I have called autobiographical are perhaps the best final index to Gertrude Stein's mind. They are, in the first place, in large degree parasitical and exploitative; while these traits are by no means the whole of her mind, they are a significant part of it. Of course, any autobiographical work is exploitative of its author's environment, but few environments have been mined more exhaustively than Miss Stein's. It seems, finally, that she capitalized on her name and on public interest in her circle of acquaintances to a point considerably beyond literature and almost beyond decency. One would at once suspect that Gertrude Stein is losing some of that integrity and obliviousness to "audience," courted so passionately in her ragged days, were it not for the fact that she palpably believes these books are good art and not mere exploitation.

The autobiographical books are singularly uneven. The one conviction they insist on, the thing the reader must accept if he is to find them of real value, is the preeminent genius of their author, the magic potency of her unique sensibility. Deny this and little remains. By and large they are chitchat—engrossing as the gossip of an alert and powerful personality who had made contact with many of the most creative people of her time. "Contact" is a distressingly accurate word here, and, if Miss Stein's own texts are to be taken as our evidence, it seems that she rarely penetrated these people and their ideas to a deeper than chitchat level. It is possible, of course, to mistake eccentricity for profundity, and it seems to me that this general error has added considerably to Gertrude Stein's reputation. In addition to being extremely interesting, her gossip is character revealing in a rather disastrous way, for it often proves to be grossly inaccurate, as Leo Stein and the authors of the "Testimony Against Gertrude Stein" have shown. The inaccuracies point to very fundamental and damaging aspects of Miss Stein's composition: her vast ego, for example, and the pathological cast of mind that allowed her memory to function in a Freudian way in order to "recall" events in those lights that always reflect glory on Gertrude Stein. Too often her accounts reveal a startling inability to comprehend the social milieu in which her own life developed.

When Miss Stein's autobiographical works attempt to probe deeply, they usually become even less satisfying. Prone to generalize widely and wildly, often without evidence or with mere eccentric shreds of fact, she almost never substantiates a theory with convincing supporting detail. Repeatedly we are asked to accept the bare ex cathedra statement and then find our own evidence in the magic of the pontifical name. Like most of her commentators, Gertrude Stein constantly begs the question.

One could cull scores of these exasperating pronouncements from her works, but her statement to a young American painter gives us a fair sample: "The minute painting gets abstract it gets pornographic."[20] This meaningless generality she supports with the bull, "That is a fact." Then she drops it and runs. But the ramifications of such a contention are enormous, and, if she is to pretend to philosophy rather than dogma, she must explore

[20] Stein, *Everybody's Autobiography*, 127.

them. A responsible thinker might have put it something like this: A painter must work with line, mass, color, light, and shade; if his work is abstract in the formal sense, it is probably true that he moves inevitably toward geometricity, working with forms—straight lines, angles, cones, cylinders, circles, ellipses—that may relate themselves subconsciously in the mind of the observer to male and female sexual equipment. If his work is abstract in its content, then he may deal primarily with the material of the subconscious, with its heavily sexual pigmentation. So far, Miss Stein's doctrine would seem to make rather good sense, although we have no way of knowing whether she arrived at it on these or better grounds.

Great questions remain. Whence comes the "pornography"? Is the prurience in the mind of the artist or in that of the observer? Mere presentation of sexuality does not constitute pornography—as Judge Woolsey fortunately ruled. If one thinks in Gertrude Stein's vein, can such a charge be leveled only at abstract art? To go to the opposite pole, how much of classical art is sex sublimated into the ideal stasis of beauty frozen or sex sublimated into the ideal kinesis of strength activated in warfare or the chase? If we are thoroughly serious, we must finally ask what proportion of the fundamental mythos of all art is sex urge. Finally, if this proportion is both large and inescapable, is it therefore pornographic? And so on. There is an unpleasant nasty-mindedness pervading this kind of thinking, an inexcusable irresponsibility in this kind of writing.

Gertrude Stein always works on the theory that being a genius relieves one of the burden of logical coherence. One need not know the mental processes of a genius; one need only accept the verbalism that results. When, however, she bares the process itself, as she occasionally does, the pattern often strikes one as startling indeed. The following lines from *Everybody's Autobiography* exemplify some of her more spectacular logic:

> ... *the most actively war-like nation the Germans always could convince the pacifists to become pro-German. That is because pacifists were such intelligent beings that they could follow what any one is saying.*
>
> *If you can follow what any one is saying then if you are a pacifist you are a pro-German. That follows if any one understands what any one is saying. Therefore understanding is a very dull occupation.*[21]

The autobiographical works share the common faults of Gertrude Stein's writing—the formlessness, the unselectiveness, the ramblings, the repetitions, the tendency to review and record all experience as unweighted "sheer phnomenon," the insistence on the value of the genius sensibility—but these matters are less painful here. They are relieved by the great liveliness of the life she lived and recorded with comparative objectivity, by much that is genuinely funny, and by the fact that she writes with a reader in mind in her noncreative—hence comprehensible

[21] *Ibid.*, 75.

—language. To adapt Miss Stein's own terms, she is serving mammon, not god, in these books; we can be grateful for her sin and follow her with understanding, if not with great profit or complete belief.

Still, if the autobiographical books record Gertrude Stein's mind at its normally functioning level, the record is one of fascinating eccentricity rather than of profundity. Hers is a mind that ranged widely and alertly, but not deeply. Here, though in less offensive degree than in her so-called creative books, the recording technique is still basically mechanical, photographic, scientific—not artistic. She records with the camera's attention to surface and with the scientist's concern for inclusiveness. The writing lacks the artist's selectiveness, his attention to drama and meaningful detail, his sense of reality rearranged into organic form. The philosophical component, though often suggestive, never develops fully; it is embryonic and thin. Stylistically, these books, too, are predominantly flat. In them we find more modeling, a higher relief, but viewed topographically, they present an absence of light and shade that is arbitrary, illogical, and symptomatic of something that once more seems very near pathology in Miss Stein's mind. The stream of reality is laid on the page exactly as it impresses the camera artist, largely unshaded and unweighed.

Gertrude Stein pursued the laboratory technician's omnivorousness and refusal to discriminate to the point where it became solidified as thinking and as technique. It may be termed pathological, and certainly it is inartistic.

An Evaluation

When experience becomes mere phenomenon, it no longer presents material for art. It is finally just to say that Gertrude Stein's true position is antiliterary, anti-intellectual, and often antihumane and antimoral. Her whole orientation is ruthlessly egocentric. Although she has defined her own ego as creative of art, she has not spoken the truth. In the market place of art, where all of us who read must work, her definition has no meaning.

We can document fully the pathology of Miss Stein's nondiscrimination. It shows itself, in varying degrees of seriousness, throughout her work. We have already noted one of its most curious manifestations in her attitude to painting: "Anything painted in oil on a flat surface" could "hold her attention." This same indiscriminate ingestiveness, this same enormous patience with triviality, presents itself in various silly but indicative situations. Carl Van Vechten testifies, for example, that she "would spend hours rearranging a box of buttons."[22] In *Everybody's Autobiography*, we find her

... hunting hazel nuts and each one I find is exciting just as much so as any other hunting. I spend long hours at it, it is very interesting.[23]

On her trip to America she was delighted by the Burma Shave "poems":

... one little piece on one board and then further on two

[22] Carl Van Vechten, Introduction to *Three Lives,* by Gertrude Stein, ix.
[23] Stein, *Everybody's Autobiography,* 114–15.

more words and then further on two more words a whole lively poem.[24]

Now certainly this kind of thing is excusable, as Gertrude Stein's apologists would insist, on the score of her gay good humor. And, no doubt, a kind of catholicity is at work here, but it is an oddly unproductive catholicity: a child's openness to experience or the openness to experience of a scientist who never grew up and who mistakes naïveté for "objectivity." With Miss Stein it is wide eyed and uncritical, and the interesting thing is the facility with which she suspends her critical faculty. For philosophy, for art, selectivity and evaluation must be added to receptiveness. Gertrude Stein believed the contrary.

The instances above typify the least unfortunate occurrences of Miss Stein's indiscriminateness. Other instances have more serious consequences. Just as there is catholicity in her hazel nuts, so there is a kind of democratizing principle in her contention that "either everything is worth writing about or nothing is worth writing about," in her insistence that she is "interested in anyone,"[25] that she prefers the normal to the abnormal,[26] that she believes in "simple middle class monotonous tradition,"[27] or that she is trying to be "as commonplace as I can be."[28] One need not be a royalist to find artistic

24 *Ibid.*, 226.
25 Stein, "Portraits and Repetition," in *Lectures in America*, 183.
26 Stein, *The Autobiography of Alice B. Toklas*, 69.
27 Stein, *The Making of Americans*, 38.
28 Stein, *The Autobiography of Alice B. Toklas*, 185–86.

perils in such a position. There can be little doubt that if the high province of art is to help us to feel and understand the pity and terror and occasional joy of being human, then the best source material for the artist lies in the commonplace and "normal"—whatever that is. Good art has unquestionably grown from the commonplace—Gertrude Stein's own *Three Lives*, for example—but it has grown because of artful selecting and proportioning and dramatizing and lyricizing, through modulation and occasional distortion. But if, as Miss Stein would have it, the commonplace is to be seen first whole and second privately, we get first dull inclusiveness and second incomprehensibility. This is not art, nor is it, finally, democracy; it is mediocrity badly communicated.

The picture of her indiscriminateness grows progressively more distasteful. Its antihumaneness and its egocentricity begin to show themselves. "One night," she says, "there was a big fire one of those nice American fires that have so many horses and firemen to attend them."[29] Experience has become sheer phenomenon indeed. Again, surely a kind of monumental detachment, though not a very pleasant one, lurks in the quality of mind that can abstract from the total horror of war everything but its impersonal movement, unpopulated by the outrage of pain and death, and equate it with a simple recreation: "That is what war is and dancing it is forward and back."[30] I do not say that Miss Stein cannot be moved by tragedy,

[29] Stein, *Everybody's Autobiography*, 143.
[30] *Ibid.*, 107.

but she can forget it if it serves her purpose of the moment. And when she is moved, she is, in all likelihood, moved because tragedy has come close to home. At the beginning of World War II, for example, she could say:

. . . we were at Béon again that Sunday, and Russia came into the war and Poland was smashed, and I did not care about Poland, but it did frighten me about France.[31]

Surely one must care about Poland, quite aside from politics, even if one lives in France.

We have seen in another context that Gertrude Stein did not believe that "causes" or intellectuality or moral distinctions of right and wrong provided the proper subject matter for art. It will be worth our while to look now at these concepts very briefly as part of her general abnormal refusal to discriminate among experiences. "Any thing that is," she believes, "is enough if it is."[32] Experience is not to be evaluated but recorded. She "does not at all mind the cause of women or any other cause but it does not happen to be her business."[33] Causes are all right, that is, for anybody else. One has only to compare Picasso's "Guernica" with Miss Stein's *Wars I Have Seen* to decide whether the human artist or the camera artist is likely to produce the better art from experience involving "causes." The same objectivity become pathology makes

[31] Gertrude Stein, "The Winner Loses," in *Selected Writings*, 543.
[32] Stein, *Everybody's Autobiography*, 6.
[33] Stein, *The Autobiography of Alice B. Toklas*, 69.

it possible for Gertrude Stein to contend that "negroes were not suffering from persecution, they were suffering from nothingness."[34]

195 Of Miss Stein's anti-intellectualism, let it suffice to remind ourselves of the outlines. Nothing tentative conditions her attitude. She says flatly, ". . . a genius need not think, because if he does think he has to be wrong or right he has to argue or decide, and after all he might just as well not do that."[35] By a simple act of assertion Miss Stein relieves herself of the burden of thought and the burden of moral choice. It should be hardly necessary to say that mere assertion of genius creates neither genius nor literature. But a great deal of Gertrude Stein's work depends upon this kind of evasion as a substitute for content.

When we turn from the autobiographical works to the specifically creative ones, those in which she is "serving god," we find ourselves in an even more barren country, the true desert. Here we are made to feel the full consequences for art of her aesthetic theories: the doctrines of spontaneous creation; the "search for immediacy" and the "whole present"; the faith in the eye rather than in the intellect, in the eye rather than in the imagination; and the progressive constricting of subject matter and technique to rule out beauty, emotion, morality, association, the subconscious, the past, all the life context surrounding the object seen—to rule out form, narrative,

[34] *Ibid.*, 196.
[35] Stein, *Everybody's Autobiography*, 86.

drama, movement, meaning; to demolish, in a word, everything not presently visible to the conglomerate eye of the camera-artist-scientist-genius and to include literally everything visible after this manner. What we get, clearly, is a drastic, almost total delimitation of the province of art; we are compensated by a multiplication of uninterpreted minutiae in the field of vision that is the artist's point of observation. This vastly elaborated triviality must then be cast in the form it stumbles into, in the unique language proper to the uniqueness of the insight.

This quick overview of the general aesthetic position of Gertrude Stein has the merit of letting us see quickly her cardinal sins: first, her attempt to revitalize the art of writing reduced itself to a destruction of all the accumulated resources of the art; second, her substitute was really no more than the narrow resources of the idiosyncratic self. The most appalling single fact about her "art" is that everything in it returns to the tinseled fiction of the pre-eminent value of the genius sensibility. The whole direction of Gertrude Stein's writing is the narrowing from public to private art, from multiplication to subtraction, from much to little.

The real content, the root matter of communication in Gertrude Stein's creative writing, may be said in general to be pathetically thin. For a writer of her supposed stature, it is quite unbelievably thin. I except, as always, *Three Lives,* written before she became Gertrude Stein. A thin but still perceptible content persists in *Ida, The Making of Americans, Things as They Are,* and

Brewsie and Willie, but this list leaves a score of volumes, the great bulk of her creative work, that have, one feels, very nearly nothing to say. When we are confronted with this fact, it is very difficult for us to understand the quantity of admiration that has been tendered Miss Stein. The truth is, one suspects, that the great mass of those who profess to admire the writings of Gertrude Stein, as apart from the personality of their creator, are unconsciously testifying not to the excellence of these writings, but to an abstract ideal, to their commitment to the civil liberty of the artist, to the premise that the artist has the right to be as eccentric as he pleases. They do not really understand what she is saying, but they wish to make very sure she is not denied the right to say it.

Few critics today would deny this right. But the reader has civil liberties, too. He has the right to deny the title of art to work that remains, after long and sympathetic immersion, unknowable and unpleasurable. There is degree in all things, including idiosyncrasy. Art moves ahead by idiosyncrasy. The strangeness of a Shakespeare, a Donne, a Coleridge, a Rabelais, a Swift, a Melville, a Proust, a Joyce—this strangeness enriches and advances literature. The strangeness of a Gertrude Stein debilitates and paralyzes. When art turns in on its creator, it may still be creation, but it is not art.

If one accepts every premise of Gertrude Stein, beginning with the great parent premise of her genius, "in english literature in her time the only one," and acquiescing all the way down through the corollaries of her complex aesthetics, there still remains the bar of language. This barrier remains final and fatal because it is the medium she has chosen, the only one through which we can apprehend her. Like her subject matter and her form, but to an even greater degree, her language is private. Gertrude Stein chose words by two main criteria: they had to have for her "existing being"—they had to be privately alive and exciting—and they did not need to be words that in general possessed objective application to the subject at hand in order to be the words that "described that thing." All of this means, practically, for the reader a vocabulary of impenetrable, esoteric abstractions. Miss Stein clearly hopes to inaugurate an art uniquely possessed of accuracy and sensitivity, evoked by words stripped of their received meanings and laid bare and new on the page—a language as new as Homer's.

It is almost incredible that a woman of Gertrude Stein's intelligence could fail to see the fallacy inherent in this position. Yet she does fail to see it, and it is this colossal blind spot that ultimately condemns her to a stillborn art. Just as her "insistence" is to us inevitably repetition, so this abstraction that she looks upon as a bright new concretion seems to us a concretion foreign to hers, based on the received meanings of the words rather than on the meanings she arbitrarily and privately assigns them. The matter is as simple as this: the words do not mean the same things to us that they mean to her; she is writing in one language, we are reading in another.

Gertrude Stein could never bring herself to see that

words are the least amenable to abstraction of all the artistic media. To a far greater degree than the musician's medium, sound, or the painter's medium, color, line, and volume, words are unseverably connected in our minds with things. When we see or hear the word, we see an image of the thing, and there is not much Miss Stein can do to make us see something else. That is why, when we read a characteristic Stein page and find that it relates itself to nothing we know, we find it easy to assume the truth of the superstition that she is aiming at abstract painterly or musical effects. Because she was inept at painting and music and because she was convinced that it was her mission to create a great abstract art—concretion by divinely inspired abstraction—she was driven to attempt an impossible degree of abstraction in the only medium left to her. She died believing she had succeeded.

The pathos and paradox of all this, as I see it, lies in the fact that the whole preoccupation with an abstract language is really unnecessary. Our language is not the abject, inadequate vessel Gertrude Stein found it to be. The real innovators—Joyce, Proust, Kafka, Hopkins, Virginia Woolf—all are constantly making the language perform new acrobatics of color, nuance, and intelligibility by sensitively exploiting with new virtuosity its ancient resources. Very fundamental questions about the quality of Miss Stein's mind therefore arise. We can dismiss her distortion of language, as Leo Stein does, as compensation for a root inadequacy with language at its everyday level, but this solution seems oversimple. There is a more complex pathology inhabiting a mind that could pursue so long and so blindly a course so pointless and so perverse.

But even if we surrender entirely, if we go not only the second mile with Gertrude Stein, but the third as well, if we grant the possibility of struggling through her words to a vague approximation of her meaning, or, failing that, of closing upon some other poor literary remnant such as "mood" or "tone," there nevertheless remains the utterly insuperable barrier of her repetition. Gertrude Stein is a ruminant animal, not with the four stomachs of the cow, but with four hundred. Committed to the doctrine that the artist must record his ongoing present knowledge of his subject, she lays each moment's perception on the page, endlessly repeating or minutely varying that of the previous moment. To say that this becomes tiresome is the grossest understatement; it is deadly, it is not art, and it is not fit fare for a sane reader.

When Gertrude Stein's votaries are forced to face the rudimentary critical question of exactly what and how much of her intent is passed on to a reader, they are generally not very enlightening in their comments. They are likely to answer with large generalities that contain what the Maine parish clerk called a flux of words and a constipation of ideas, or, if they are trapped into being specific, the consequences are sometimes amusing. Julian Sawyer, for example, in his confident exegesis of the famous "rose" line, saw a yellow rose.[36] It must have been embarrassing to have his yellow rose become, in Miss

[36] Sawyer, *op. cit.*, 16.

Stein's own explanation of the line, "red for the first time in English poetry for a hundred years."[37] The initiated Mr. Sawyer is no better off than the carping critic who sees only the same old limp pink rambler he always sees when he hears the word "rose." W. H. Gardner read Miss Stein's "Susie Asado" as a portrait of "an amiable, slip-shod, canary-bright spinster,"[38] but Carl Van Vechten, who should know, says that the piece is a portrait of a Spanish flamenco dancer.[39] How mistaken can one be?

What usually happens, it would appear, is that Gertrude Stein's readers find something emerging to them and seize it thankfully and assume in self-defense that it is the thing she meant them to receive; otherwise, all is chaos. But the uncomely truth is that all, or very nearly all, *is* chaos. Very little that is real or tangible passes from Gertrude Stein to the reader. Actual meeting of minds or sensibilities rarely takes place. The single weighable, measurable function of her most characteristic works is their service as a simple irritant. They say, in effect, "Think about this thing I have named"—little more. Generally, if value accrues, it develops in the reader's variation on the theme, not in Miss Stein's.

If Gertrude Stein would only admit the poverty of her content and admit that its essential quality is vague suggestion, she would be a great deal more respectable. But she would confess neither. Because the content of her

[37] Wilder, Introduction to *Four In America,* by Gertrude Stein, vi.

[38] Gardner, *op. cit.*, 269.

[39] Van Vechten, in *Selected Writings,* 485.

writing was the content of the genius vision, it was to be considered always dense and ponderable. She stubbornly insisted that her object was always concretely present on

the page; if communication was imperfect, that was the fault of the reader. So she grumbles, "Mostly those to whom I am explaining are not completely hearing,"[40] and, more heatedly, "But what's the difficulty? Just read the words on the paper. They're in English. Just read them. Be simple and you'll understand these things."[41]

The amazing thing is that this is perfectly honest mystification and outrage. Gertrude Stein seems never to have understood certain elementary facts: that it is impossible to be "simple" with English words because they are loaded with meaning; that she is speaking one language, we another; that it is never possible for one mind to know another really well, impossible for one to know another at all without help. Therefore, it is accurate to say that throughout her creative life, Gertrude Stein practiced a kind of cultivated schizophrenia. By an act that may have been will, or stupidity, or some curious pathological quirk, she convinced herself first of the inevitable rightness of her position and then of the inevitable communicability of her vision through the chosen language. Willfully, or stupidly, or pathologically, she blinded herself to the crusted connotativeness of language and to the insularity of sensibilities foreign to her own. She sealed these unpalatable truths in a compartment of her brain that she

[40] Stein, *The Making of Americans*, 315.
[41] Wilder, Introduction to *Four in America*, by Gertrude Stein, v.

never again entered. She takes an idea that could be made clear and cold in expository prose, or clear and warm in narrative-dramatic prose, or warm and vaguely—perhaps
 more meaningfully—clear in intelligible abstraction, and makes it cold and unclear—dead—in unintelligible abstraction. So I see the matter.

I am inclined to contend, then, that Gertrude Stein's creative writings are undernourished in intrinsic matter, that even this poverty fails of communication by being cast in a foreign language, and that her works are therefore practically worthless as art.

Since we have already discounted Miss Stein's autobiographical works as largely unselective chitchat, taking their principal value from their revelation of eccentricity, we are left with only her critical-aesthetic writings. The best of Gertrude Stein appears in these lectures. In them she tries her best to be serious and philosophical and plainly intelligible, and, with some reservations, she succeeds. She is wholly serious and genuinely, but not always deeply or originally, philosophical. The degree of her intelligibility depends on the reader's patience and the quantity of his previous exposure to Miss Stein's thinking and linguistic habits; with some experience and much patience, the reader can know her in all her lectures.

I have already discussed the content of the lectures at great length, and there is no need to go through it all again. Here we need only make the point that in them Gertrude Stein shows a mind that is not great, but it is good enough to point up by contrast the pathos of her failure as an artist. The texts of the lectures often dramatize this failure in a very interesting and conclusive way: the occurrence there of the phenomenon in which Miss Stein, after making an eloquent and intricate presentation of one of her theories, pauses to read from her creative works to demonstrate the art that follows from the theory just expounded. The result, generally, is not enlightenment but blank mystification. The thing that had seemed interesting and worth while as theory has become perfectly opaque as art.

The best of her lectures are "Composition as Explanation," "What Are Masterpieces," "How Writing Is Written," "Plays," and "Poetry and Grammar." Her "Narration" lectures at the University of Chicago deal heavily in trivia and contain much that is repetition of earlier material. Of the four lectures in addition to "Plays" and "Poetry and Grammar" that are collected in *Lectures in America*, "What Is English Literature" and "Pictures" are almost completely unrewarding, casting serious doubt, as I have said, on the depth of Miss Stein's critical perceptions in the arts generally. "The Gradual Making of The Making of Americans" and "Portraits and Repetition," unevenly interesting, have value largely as exposition of Miss Stein's private literary practices.

These lectures, in contrast to the creative writings, hold more gold than dross, but we need not pretend to agree that the gold in them entitles Gertrude Stein to the title of genius she claims and in which she is supported by her admirers. But certainly enough may be found to defend her from the charge of being a fool and a charlatan, charges that have been leveled by her vilifiers. There is no point in vilifying Gertrude Stein. She is the victim of her pathology rather than her villainy. Her powers as an aesthetic theorist seem considerably better than mediocre, considerably less than first rate. Whatever its idiosyncrasy, her system is perfectly coherent. Against much that strikes one as mistaken or merely trivial must be set much that is interesting as theory and potentially fruitful for others, if not for herself. In her aesthetics Miss Stein is no more derivative than in her artistic practice, and one can almost always trace the maturing of an idea through her own thinking rather than through another's. Whatever Gertrude Stein is, she is self-made.

The two most interesting attitudes that emerge from the lectures are her passionate concern for the integrity of the artist and her doctrine of the necessary "presentness" of the ideal creative state. Nothing shows more painfully the drastic disparity between Gertrude Stein's aesthetics and her art than an examination of the product of these doctrines in her practice. When she moves to translate them into art, her schizophrenia goes to work and she blinds herself to proportion, to the necessity of compromising the ideal and the real. To maintain integrity, Miss Stein felt that she had to make herself not merely honest but unique; being unique, she is unknowable, and her creation is stillborn. To maintain the "presentness" of the creative vision, she threw away the archives, closed her mind and her conscience, fixed her lens in a static position, photographed reality as a still-life succession, and then ran the film through a warped projector onto the standard screen of the printed page. The result is a flawed art by subtraction and abstraction.

Gertrude Stein is not alone, of course, in being concerned with the illumination of the present moment of consciousness. This might with justice be called the characteristic preoccupation of prose writers in our time. The greatest of her contemporaries devoted major portions of their careers to its solution. Compared with them, she is pathetic—no other word suffices. To her pathetic narrowing must be compared their burgeoning inclusiveness; to her fortuitous form, their organic form; to her art-for-art insulation from life, their hot immersion in it; to her drab, cacophonous emptiness, their proliferation of the possibilities for beauty, meaning, and passion in the language. Gertrude Stein is right, as the others are right, in believing that it is important that art illuminate the "complete actual present," but in her method she is terrifically, fatally wrongheaded. Joyce once suggested that readers should devote their lives to his works, and his suggestion is less than absurd. But the feeling that remains after reading Gertrude Stein is not one of illumination and profit, but one of darkness and waste.

After writing *The Making of Americans*, Gertrude Stein should have made the great confession and begun anew. Instead, she burrowed blindly, molewise, deeper into a cul-de-sac. Now, reading her books, one lists the good things of literature and crosses them off one by one:

her works possess no beauty, no instruction, no passion. All that is finally there is Gertrude Stein mumbling to herself. Everything in her writing returns upon the self for value. All that is left of literature is its function as delight to its creator—which perhaps justifies its writing, but not its being put in print.

Gertrude Stein, it seems to me, is already effectively dead as a writer. Nobody really reads her, but everybody continues to talk knowingly and concernedly about her. Her "importance" is a myth. She is enormously interesting as a phenomenon of the power of personality and as a symptom of a frantic, fumbling, nightmare age—our present—and it is as such that she will live. Later ages will gather about the corpus of her work like a cluster of horrified medical students around a biological sport.

BIBLIOGRAPHY

THE WRITINGS OF GERTRUDE STEIN

Geography and Plays. Boston, Four Seas Company, 1922.

Useful Knowledge. London, Bodley Head, Ltd., n.d.

Lucy Church Amiably. Paris, Imprimerie "Union," 1930.

How to Write. Paris, 1931. Plain edition.

Matisse Picasso and Gertrude Stein. Paris, 1933. Plain edition.

Three Lives. New York, Modern Library, 1933.

The Making of Americans. New York, Harcourt, Brace and Company, 1934. Abridged edition.

Portraits and Prayers. New York, Random House, 1934.

Lectures in America. New York, Random House, 1935.

Narration. Chicago, University of Chicago Press, 1935.

The Geographical History of America or the Relation of Human Nature to the Human Mind. New York, Random House, 1936.

Everybody's Autobiography. New York, Random House, 1937.

Paris, France. New York, Charles Scribner's Sons, 1940.

What Are Masterpieces. Los Angeles, Conference Press, 1940.

Ida. New York, Random House, 1941.

Wars I Have Seen. New York, Random House, 1945.

The Autobiography of Alice B. Toklas. In *Selected Writings of Gertrude Stein, q. v.*

Selected Writings of Gertrude Stein. Edited by Carl Van Vechten. New York, Random House, 1946.

Brewsie and Willie. New York, Random House, 1946.

Four in America. New Haven, Yale University Press, 1947.

Blood on the Dining Room Floor. New York, Banyan Press, 1948.

Last Operas and Plays. Edited by Carl Van Vechten. New York and Toronto, Rinehart and Company, 1949.

Things as They Are. New York, Banyan Press, 1950.

(The Yale edition of the unpublished writings of Gertrude Stein, under the general editorship of Carl Van Vechten, with an advisory committee of Donald C. Gallup, Donald Sutherland, and Thornton Wilder, published by Yale University Press, New Haven, follows.)

Two: Gertrude Stein and Her Brother and Other Early Portraits. With a foreword by Janet Flanner. 1951.

Mrs. Reynolds and Five Earlier Novelettes. With a foreword by Lloyd Frankenberg. 1952.

Bee Time Vine and Other Pieces. With a preface and notes by Virgil Thomson. 1953.

As Fine as Melanctha. With a foreword by Natalie Clifford Barney. 1954.

Painted Lace and Other Pieces. With an introduction by Daniel-Henry Kahnweiler. 1955.

Stanzas in Meditation and Other Poems. With a preface by Donald Sutherland. 1956.

Alphabets and Birthdays. With an introduction by Donald Gallup. 1957.

BOOKS

Anderson, Margaret. *My Thirty Years' War.* New York, Covici, Friede, 1930.

Benét, William Rose, and Norman Holmes Pearson (eds.). *The Oxford Anthology of American Literature.* New York, Oxford University Press, 1941. 2 vols.

Brooks, Van Wyck. *Opinions of Oliver Allston.* New York, E. P. Dutton and Company, 1941.

Canby, Henry Seidel. *American Estimates.* New York, Harcourt, Brace and Company, 1929.

Cargill, Oscar. *Intellectual America.* New York, The Macmillan Company, 1941.

Cowley, Malcolm (ed.). *After the Genteel Tradition.* New York, W. W. Norton and Company, 1937.

Eastman, Max. *The Literary Mind.* New York and London, Charles Scribner's Sons, 1935.

Gallup, Donald Clifford (ed.). *The Flowers of Friendship: Letters Written to Gertrude Stein.* New York, Alfred A. Knopf, 1953.

Gardner, W. H. *Gerard Manley Hopkins*. New Haven, Yale University Press, 1948.

Haas, Robert Bartlet, and Donald Clifford Gallup. *A Catalogue of the Published and Unpublished Writings of Gertrude Stein*. New Haven, Yale University Press, 1941.

Imbs, Bravig. *Confessions of Another Young Man*. New York, Henkle-Yewdale House, Inc., 1936.

James, William. *Essays in Radical Empiricism*. New York, Longmans, Green and Company, 1912.

———. *The Philosophy of William James*. New York, Modern Library, 1925.

———. *Psychology*. New York, Henry Holt and Company, 1893.

Lewis, Wyndham. *Time and Western Man*. New York, Harcourt, Brace and Company, 1928.

MacCarthy, Desmond. *Criticism*. London, Putnam, 1932.

Miller, Rosamond S. *Gertrude Stein: Form and Intelligibility*. New York, Exposition Press, 1949.

Putnam, Samuel. *Paris Was Our Mistress*. New York, The Viking Press, 1947.

Rogers, W. G. *When This You See Remember Me*. New York, Rinehart and Company, 1948.

Rosenfeld, Paul. *By Way of Art*. New York, Coward-McCann, 1928.

Sawyer, Julian. *Gertrude Stein: A Bibliography*. New York, Arrow Editions, 1940.

Sherman, Stuart Pratt. *Points of View*. New York, Charles Scribner's Sons, 1924.

Sitwell, Edith. *Poetry and Criticism. (The Hogarth Essays, XI.)* London, Hogarth Press, 1925.

Sprigge, Elizabeth. *Gertrude Stein: Her Life and Her Work*. New York, Harper and Brothers, 1957.

Stein, Leo. *Journey into the Self*. Edited by Edmund Fuller. New York, Crown Publishers, 1950.

Sutherland, Donald. *Gertrude Stein: A Biography of Her Work*. New Haven, Yale University Press, 1951.

Whitehead, Alfred North. *Science and the Modern World*. New York, Pelican Mentor Books, 1948.

Wilson, Edmund. *Axel's Castle*. New York, Charles Scribner's Sons, 1931.

ARTICLES

Aiken, Conrad. "We Ask for Bread," *New Republic,* Vol. LXXVIII (April 4, 1934), 219.

Alsop, Joseph. "Gertrude Stein on Writing," *New York Herald Tribune Books,* January 10, 1937, 2.

Auden, W. H. "All About Ida," *Saturday Review of Literature,* Vol. XXIII (February 22, 1941), 8.

Bernstein, Leonard. "Music and Miss Stein," *New York Times Book Review,* May 22, 1949, 4, 22.

Braque, Georges, Eugene Jolas, Maria Jolas, Henri Matisse, André Salmon, and Tristan Tzara. "Testimony Against Gertrude Stein," Supplement to *transition,* Vol. XXIII (July, 1935).

Bromfield, Louis. "Gertrude Stein, Experimenter with Words," *New York Herald Tribune Books,* September 3, 1933, 1–2.

Burke, Kenneth. "Engineering with Words," *Dial*, Vol. LXXIV (April, 1923), 408–12.

———. "The Impartial Essence," *New Republic*, Vol. LXXXIII (July 3, 1935), 227.

———. "Two Brands of Piety," *Nation*, Vol. CXXXVIII (February 28, 1934), 256–58.

Canby, Henry Seidel. "Cheating at Solitaire," *Saturday Review of Literature*, Vol. XI (November 17, 1934), 290.

Chamberlain, Dorothy. "Gertrude Stein, Amiably," *New Republic*, Vol. CIV (April 7, 1941), 477.

Chew, Samuel. "O Heart, Rise Not Up Against Me as a Witness," *Yale Review*, Vol. XXIII (Winter, 1934), 392–93.

Eagleson, Harvey. "Gertrude Stein; Method in Madness," *Sewanee Review*, Vol. XLIV (1936), 164–77.

Fadiman, Clifton. "Getting Gertie's Ida," *New Yorker*, Vol. XVII (February 15, 1941), 66.

Fay, Bernard. "A Rose Is a Rose," *Saturday Review of Literature*, Vol. X (September 2, 1933), 77–79.

Fitts, Dudley. "Toasted Susie Is My Ice-Cream," *New York Times Book Review*, November 30, 1947, 5.

"Flat Prose," *Atlantic Monthly*, Vol. CXIV (September, 1914), 430–32.

Flint, F. Cudworth. "Contemporary Criticism," *Southern Review*, Vol. II (1936–1937), 208–13.

Fremantle, Anne. "Mom in the Kitchen," *Commonweal*, Vol. XLV (October 25, 1946), 33–35.

"Gertrude Stein and a Robin," *Atlantic Monthly,* Vol. CXXXIII (March, 1924), 427–28.

Haines, George IV. "Forms of Imaginative Prose: 1900–1940," *Southern Review,* Vol. VII (Spring, 1942), 755.

Krutch, Joseph Wood. "A Prepare for Saints," *Nation,* Vol. CXXXVIII (April 4, 1934), 396, 398.

Lerman, Leo. "A Wonderchild for 72 Years," *Saturday Review of Literature,* Vol. XXIX (November 2, 1946), 7–18.

Marini, Myra. "Being Dead Is Something," *New Republic,* Vol. LXXXIX (January 20, 1937), 365.

Miller, Perry. "Steinese," *New York Times Book Review,* November 3, 1946, 6, 30.

Moore, Marianne. "The Spare American Emotion," *Dial,* Vol. LXXX (February, 1926), 153–56.

Norman, Sylva. "Words and Waste," *Nation and Athenaeum,* Vol. XLV (April 13, 1929), 52.

Paulding, C. G. "Let Them Talk and Talk," *Commonweal,* Vol. XLIV (August 2, 1946), 384–85.

Preston, John Hyde. "A Conversation," *Atlantic Monthly,* Vol. CLVI (August, 1935), 187–94.

Rascoe, Burton. "Self-Confidential," *Saturday Review of Literature,* Vol. XVII (December 4, 1937), 11.

Redman, Ben Ray. "Word-Intoxicated Woman," *Saturday Review of Literature,* Vol. XXXII (April 2, 1949), 18–19.

Riding, Laura. "The New Barbarism and Gertrude Stein," *transition,* Vol. III (June, 1927), 153–68.

Skinner, B. F. "Has Gertrude Stein a Secret?" *Atlantic Monthly,* Vol. CLIII (January, 1934), 50.

Stein, Gertrude. "Cultivated Motor Automatism," *Psychological Review,* Vol. V (May, 1898), 295–306.

———. "Plays and Landscapes," *Saturday Review of Literature,* Vol. XI (November 10, 1934), 269–70.

———, and Leon Solomons. "Normal Motor Automatism," *Psychological Review,* Vol. III (September, 1896), 492–513.

"Three Lives," *Nation,* Vol. XC (January 20, 1910), 65.

Troy, William. "A Note on Gertrude Stein," *Nation,* Vol. CXXXVII (September 6, 1933), 274–75.

"Useful Knowledge," *New Statesman,* Vol. XXXIII (April 13, 1929), 22.

Van Ghent, Dorothy. "Gertrude Stein and the Solid World." In *American Stuff.* New York, The Viking Press, 1937.

Wilcox, Wendell. "A Note on Stein and Abstraction," *Poetry,* Vol. LV (February, 1940), 254–57.

Wilson, Edmund. "Brewsie and Willie," *New Yorker,* Vol. XXII (June 15, 1946), 92.

INDEX

An unconventional typographic design seemed appropriate for a book about an unconventional person. In

ART BY SUBTRACTION

there are two departures from traditional handling. The first is the use of sans serif types (types without terminating strokes) for display on the title page and for chapter heads. The faces used are Bauer Venus Extra Bold Extended and Linotype Gothic.

The second departure from convention is the use of unusually placed margins.

For the text type, W. A. Dwiggins' Electra was chosen because of its air of crisp modernity.

UNIVERSITY OF OKLAHOMA PRESS